Rouen

ITS HISTORY

AND

MONUMENTS.

ROUEN
ÆDWARD FRÈRE
1840

L

Rouen.

Lk⁷ 8379

Price : 2 Francs.

IN THE PRESS:

Histoire du Parlement de Normandie, précédée d'un Essai historique sur l'échiquier; par A. Floquet. 6 vols. 8vo. Price, 36 fr.

Chronique des Abbés de Saint-Ouen, publiée d'après un MS. de la Bibliothèque du Roi, par Francisque Michel. 4to, with a view of the abbey. Price, 10 fr.

Printed by I.-S. LEFÈVRE, successor to F. BAUDRY, 20, rue des Carmes, Rouen.

Rouen.

ROUEN,
ITS HISTORY AND MONUMENTS;
A
GUIDE TO STRANGERS.

BY THÉOD. LICQUET,

MEMBER OF THE ROYAL ACADEMY OF ROUEN, ETC.

With a Map of the Town and five Views.

ABRIDGED, AND TRANSLATED FROM THE FRENCH

BY M. D. C.

ROUEN:

EDWARD FRÈRE, QUAI DE PARIS,

Near the suspension Bridge.

MDCCC XL.

Rouen.

HISTORICAL INTRODUCTION.

Cæsar, in his Commentaries does not
speak of Rouen ; Pomponius Mela, does
not mention it in his Geography; Ptolemy is
the first author who has noticed it. This observation alone will shew the absurdity of
the numerous etymologies assigned to its
name of Rothomagus, of which we have
made Rouen. The least unlikely are those
which have been taken from the primitive
language of the country ; but, even then
we can only form conjectures more or less

1

vague, as, in deriving Rothomagus from
two celtic words, some have considered that
this name signifies a great town ; others, a
town on the bank of a river ; while others
again a town where duties were paid.

Ptolemy then gives us a commencement
to the history of Rouen. In his lifetime,
that is to say, during the first part of the
second-century, Rouen bore the name of
Rothomagus ; it was the capital of the country of the Velocasses.

If Rouen, as a town of Gaul, is little know,
to us, Rouen as a Roman town is more so. Its
existence is no longer doubtful ; its importance even is proved. All suppositions join
to make one think that the Romans were the
first who erected external fortifications round
the town. Remains of walls evidently built
by that people, were discovered in 1789 in
the cellars of a house which had been built
on the edge of the first ditch[1]. These buildings extended westward even under the

church of Saint-Lo, and it is very probable that they joined towards the east with other remains of roman architecture, found in digging the foundations of another house, n° 2, rue de la Châine.

Here then, is the first boundary of Rouen under the Romans, and drawn out by them : *on the south* the Seine, the waters of which at this time came as high as the line occupied at present by the rue des Bonnetiers, the place de la Câlende, that of Notre-Dame on its southern portion, and thus along to the extremity of the rue aux Ours. *On the north,* the ditch which existed the whole length of the streets de l'Aumône, and Fossés-Louis-VIII, that is to say, from the river Robec at the east, to the rue de la Poterne at the west. From the latter point draw a line in

---

' It is the sugar refinery of M᾿ Sautelet, rue des Carmes, opposite the place of the same name.

a southern direction passing across the New-
Market, the rue Massacre and the rue des
Vergetiers, to the rue aux Ours and you will
have the *western limit*. The *eastern limit*
is naturally marked out by the course of the
Robec. The town maintained this boundary
till the Xth century, the period of the establishment of Rollon, in this portion of Neus-
tria to which the Normans gave their name.

I have already said, that Rouen, was an
important town under the Romans, and this
truth is proved by the fact. It does not figures, it is true, in the notice of the digni-
ties of the Empire, as the seat of a superior
magistrate, but, nevertheless it is spoken
of, as a town having a garrison; and, it was
there that the *præfectus militum Ursariensium*
or, as we should say in English, the colonel
of the regiment of the Ursarians, resided.

The ecclesiastical annals also prove the
importance of Rouen at this period. We
find, in fact, during the first ages of christia-

nity, the apostles coming into Gaul, going to Rouen, and fixing their abode in a principal town that the sacred word might be more easily spread thro' the surrounding country.

As Saint-Nicaise did not come to Rouen, we must consider Saint-Mellon, as its most ancient bishop. The erection, or the consecration of a first chapel in Rouen, under the patronage of the virgin, is the only important event which the life of this prelate contains. As to the destruction of a temple dedicated to the pretended idol Roth, I think I have proved in an other work [1], first, that there never existed an idol of that name, neither was the temple situated on the ground occupied by the church of Saint-Lo; secondly, that this temple was demolished by Saint-Romain, nearly four hundred years later.

---

[1] *Recherches sur l'histoire religieuse, morale et littéraire de Rouen, depuis les premiers temps jusqu'à Rollon.* Rouen, J. Frère, 1826, 8vo.

1.

Nothing very remarkable happened at Rouen, under the successors of Saint-Mellon, until Saint-Victrice. But, here commences a new era for the town. Its population increases, its reputation extends, the temples of the true god are multiplied; even Saint-Victrice himself works in their erection : « He rolls the stones with his own hands, he carries them on his shoulders. »

This town continued its career peaceably during nearly a century, until Saint-Godard succeeded to the episcopate. Then we come to a great historical transition.

Roman power had been long struggling against the encroachments of the Francs in Gaul. Clovis, conquers the provinces situated between the Somme, the Seine and the Aisne ; the monarchy commences, and Rouen becomes a French town.

To Saint-Godard who died in 529, Flavius succeeded the same year. The first foundation by Clotaire I, of the abbey of

Saint–Peter, now Saint–Ouen, about the year 540, is attributed to him.

After Flavius, came Pretextat, whose name alone reminds us of those of two women, unfortunately too celebrated, Fredégonde and Brunehaut. The latter had been exiled to Rouen, by Chilperic, king of Soissons. Merovee, son of Chilperic, loved Brunehaut and was loved by her. He came to Rouen, and married his mistress; Pretextat blessed their union. Chilperic arrives and the two lovers take refuge in the church of Saint–Martin–sur–Renelle, a wooden building, on the wall of the town. It is to Gregory of Tours that we owe this information which is valuable, in as much, as it makes us acquainted with the limits of Rouen on the north–west side at this period.

Fredegonde did not pardon Pretextat; she caused him to be murdered, during mass, in the Cathedral.

The episcopate of Melance and of Hidulfe,

the successors to Pretextat, offers no very
particular circumstances. That of Saint-
Romain, is much more remarkable, for the
destruction of heathen temples, and the
famous miracle of the *Gargouille*, which,
gave birth to the privilege not less famous,
which the chapter possessed of setting at
liberty a prisoner every year. It is thought
generally, however, that Saint-Romain,
constructed one of the churches, which
succeeded each other on the site of the
Cathedral, but, they were decieved who
have said that this bishop extirpated paga-
nism from Rouen, and from the province.
Saint-Ouen, who came after Saint-Romain,
found the people clownish, superstitious,
and idolatrous, in consequence of the negli-
gence of some bishops, his predecessors.
The inhabitants of the neighbouring country,
were coarse, cruel and dishonest; morals
and the sciences were cultivated only among
the higher classes of society. We find in the

preface to the life of Saint-Eloi by Saint-
Ouen, that, even in the VIIth century, they
read authors of whose works nothing now
remains.

Saint-Ouen, founded or enriched a great
many religious establishments in Rouen and
its environs. It was under his episcopate, that
a monument was first raised to Saint-Nicaise
within the walls of Rouen. He also caused
to be built the celebrated abbeys of Fontenelle (since Saint-Wandrille), Jumiéges, and
Saint-Austreberthe.

In the time of this archbishop, there
was a state prison near the end of the rue
de la Poterne. It was in this prison that
Saint – Ouen, having been deceived by
the mayor of the palace Ebroin, caused
Philibert the first Abbot of Jumieges to be
confined on a false accusation of the crime of
high-treason.

To Saint-Ouen, Ansbert succeeded in
683; at this time doubtless the mechanical

arts were not very far advanced in Rouen,
since the new bishop, wishing to erect a
rich mausoleum to his predecessor, sent for
workmen from different provinces.

According to the monk Aigrad, a great
famine took place in Rouen and its neighbourhood, during the episcopate of Ansbert,
who caused the treasures of the church to
be given, for the relief of the poor.

Here, the history of Rouen is lost in
obscurity; our materials are reduced, we
may almost say, to the mere list of bishops,
until the time when the north—men shewed
themselves in this country. From the year
841, when they appeared for the first time
at the mouth of the Seine, until the year
912, the period of the treaty of Saint-
Claire-sur-Epte, Rouen, and its environs
presented nothing but a scene of carnage,
fire, and, slaughter. Strangers devouring
the country; the villages deserted; the population massacred; the towns half des-

troyed, every where discord, hatred, ava
rice, and rapacity; all excesses united :
such is the picture of the country at that
period. At last Rollo, is created duke of
Normandy; the proud Norwegian, becomes
the benefactor of the country, to which he
had so long proved a scourge. The population reappears; an active police is established, robberies are put a stop to; no
more plunderers exist on the highways, or
thieves in the towns. Rouen, rises from
amidst its ruins, its monuments are repaired, its size increases, its political in-
fluence is becoming immense.

The second boundary is due to Rollo,
the first duke, and to his son Guillaume
Longue-Epée. They confined the waters
of the Seine in a narrower bed. Several
churches, such as Saint-Martin-de-la-
Roquette, Saint-Clement, Saint-Stephen
and Saint-Eloi, which had till then been
situated on small islands, were united to

the main land , the portion which had been
gained from the river, received the name
of *Terres—Neuves*. The limits of the town
remained the same on the north, east and
west.

Under the first succeeding dukes , the
town extended westward , as far as the
Old—Market place. The *porte Cauchoise*
was erected about the begining of the XIth
century, that is to say, under Richard II.

The fourth boundary was effected under
the last dukes. The town extended on the
north to the height of the rue Pincedos : on
the east, to the rue de la Chèvre. These two
streets occupy the ground on which the
ditches were situated at that time.

A very short time after, Philip—Augustus,
who had just taken Rouen, and all Normandy
from Jean—Sans—Terre , caused the old castle
to be built, which was included within
the interior of the town, in the middle
of the XIIIth century; the fifth boundary was

made in the reign of Saint-Louis. Rouen was
then enlarged by the greater portion of the
ground which forms the parishes of Saint-
Patrice, Saint-Nicaise, Saint-Vivien, and
Saint-Maclou. The gates of Martainville,
Saint-Hilaire and Bouvreuil were then
built.

A sixth enlargement took place about the
middle of the XIV th century. The monastery of the Jacobins, which now forms a
portion of the prefecture, was enclosed
within the walls of the town, as also the
Church of Saint-Peter-le-Portier, so that it
obliged them to put the porte Cauchoise
farther out. On the east, the town was enlarged by the quarter of the Marequerie.

It is not probably to Rollo, the first duke
that we owe the institution of the exchequer.
The first trace of it, is only found under
William-the-Conqueror. Perhaps even, it
was only known under his son Henry I st « the
King Duke. » Ancient writers have thought

2

that an exchequer existed in England before
the conquest. The learned Madox, on the
contrary, (vol. 1st page 177 and following)
declares, that he has not found in any
document prior to William's expedition ,
the word *scaccarium* (or *exchequer*) But he
finds it shortly after that time, from which it
would appear natural to conclude that, that
institution had been carried over by that
prince. The exchequer was removed sometimes to Rouen, at other times to Caen, and
sometimes to Falaise. Louis XIIth fixed
this sovereign court at Rouen, in 1449, and
opened it on the 1st october of the same
year. Francis Ist raised the exhecquer into
a parliament in the year 1515. It was
interdicted in the month of August 1540,
but the 7th January 1541, was reinstated.

Thick walls, deep ditches, and formidable
towers, a great many turrets , bastions , ca-
semates, and fortified gates, made Rouen an
important place, before the revolution :

omitting the different sieges, which it had to
sustain from the Normans, we must notice
in 949 those by Otho, emperor of Germany,
Louis IVth, king of France, and Arnould
count of Flanders; that in 1204 by Philip-
Augustus, 1418, by Henry V^th king of
England; that in 1449, after which,
Charles VIIth retook the town from the
English; lastly, that of 1591, by Henry IVth.
In all these sieges, and many more which I
have not mentioned, the inhabitants of Rouen
always gave proofs of great valour and
sometimes of a resignation without example.

All the fortifications of the town have
disappeared since the revolution; its ancient
appearance, is now only found in the interior, in its religious monuments and a few
houses, which time or the hand of man appears to have forgotten.

Before 1790, Rouen contained thirty
seven parochial churches and about as many
religious communities of both sexes. It now

only contains six parochial churches, and
eight chapels of ease, with a church for the
use of protestants.

Rouen is situated on a gentle slope, on
the right bank of the Seine, which forms
the southern boundary; the suburb of Saint-
Sever, is situated on the left bank. The
geographical position of the town is the 49°
26' 27'' of north latitude and 1° 14' 16''
longitude, from the meridian of Paris. The
sun rises and sets about five minutes later
at Rouen, than at Paris. The length of
Rouen without the suburbs, is one kilometre
and three hundred metres, or about the third
part of a league, from the south extremity
of the rue Grand—Pont, to the north extremity of the rue Beauvoisine. Its length from
east to west is a quarter of a league, from one
extremity to the other of the places Cauchoise and Saint-Hilaire. The circumference
of the town by the quays does not exceed six
kilometres or one league and a half.

Rouen, by its home and foreign trade, is one of the most important towns of the kingdom ; the numerous manufactories which it contains, have caused it to be surnamed the Manchester of France[1]. Rouen, is the see of an archbishopric, whose metropolitan church has for suffragans the bishoprics of Bayeux, Evreux, Seez and Coutances. It is the chief place of the fourteenth military division ; the principal town of the departement of the Seine-Inferieure.

There is besides at Rouen, a cour royale, a tribunal de première instance, six courts of justices of the peace ; a chamber and tri-

---

[1] The principal filatures, manufactories and bleaching establishements , are situated in the suburb of Saint-Sever, and in the valleys of Deville , Bapeaume and Maromme. Amongst the principal stuffs, which are wrought in its manufactories, we must mention its *rouenneries* , the general name given to all those striped or checked cotton, stuffs which are used for womens dresses.

2.

bunal of commerce, a counsel of prudent
men for the arbitration of small differences,
principally between the manufacturers and
their workmen; boards of direction for the
direct and indirect taxes, for the customs
and for the registry of domains, and a mint.
Amonsgt the principal public buildings are two
large hospitals, a handsome custom-house,
the exchange, a magnificent lunatic asylum
(in Saint-Sever), a large and small seminary,
a royal college, nineteen public schools, a
great many elementary schools for children
of both sexes, and two principal prisons.

Lastly, this town has thirty three barriers,
three covered markets, eight open markets,
twenty one public places, about seventeen
thousand houses, and more than four hundred and seventy streets, and contains a
population of about ninety thousand inhabitants.

Cathédrale.

●●

RELIGIOUS MONUMENTS.

PAROCHIAL CHURCHES.

CATHEDRAL.

All historians attribute the erection, or at least the consecration of the first christian chapel in Rouen to Saint–Mellon. They agree also in placing that chapel on a portion of the ground occupied at present by the Cathedral. To point out exactly the place, would be next to impossible; but we must necessarily suppose it to the north end of the present edifice. The tower of Saint–Romain, the foundation of which is probably the remains of one of the churches

which succeeded each other on this spot, and
which, is assuredly the most ancient part
of the whole edifice, would of itself, prove
what I say. It will not be doubted, when
we remember that the waters of the Seine,
during the time of Saint-Mellon (260 to 311),
and even seven centuries afterwards, reached as high as the place, which is known
at present by the name of *la Calende*, that
is to say almost at the base of the present
Cathedral on its southern side.

The Cathedral, which was pillaged in the
year 841, was not, according to all probabi-
lity, destroyed then; or, we must suppose
(that which is hardly possible), that it had
been rebuilt in the interval before the year
912, the period of the baptism of Rollo in
this church. Being exposed to continual acts
of devastation from pirates, the inhabitants
fled in all directions, and did not think of
building temples; and as Rollo, having been
baptized in this Cathedral, in the year 912,

made most magnificent presents immediately after the ceremony, it is clear, that the
edifice had been only plundered and not
destroyed.

About the end of the Xth century, Richard I[st] caused the Cathedral to be enlarged.
The archbishop Robert continued the impro-
vements.

Guillaume–le–Bâtard placed Maurille in
the archiepiscopal see, in the year 1055.
Maurille finished the Cathedral, and caused
to be erected the stone pyramid which bears
his name, and in the year 1063, he dedicated
the temple in the presence of William, and
the bishops of Bayeux, Avranches, Lisieux,
Evreux, Seez and Coutances.

In 1119, this Cathedral was struck by the
electric fluid.

In 1200, the metropolitan church was destroyed by fire. Jean–Sans–Terre, duke of
Normandy and king of England, assigned
funds for the reconstruction of the edifice.

It is then from that period that the actual Cathedral dates.

I need not add that this immense edifice, such as we see it at present, is the work of several centuries, beginning in the XIIIth and finishing in the XVIth, excepting that portion which forms the base of the tower of Saint-Romain, and which is much more ancient.

. The length of the Cathedral, in the inside, from the great portal to the extremity of the chapel of the Virgin, is four hundred and eight feet (about four hundred and fifty english); the chapel of the virgin is eighty eight feet in length; the choir is one hundred and ten, and the nave two hundred and ten. The entire breadth of the edifice from one wall to the other is ninety seven feet two inches; namely, the nave twenty seven feet; thickness of each pillar, seven feet eight inches, each aisle fourteen feet, the chapels thirteen feet five inches.

The height of the nave is eighty four feet; that of the aisles is forty two feet, the transept is one hundred and sixty four feet in length, by twenty six in breadth. In the centre is a lantern, at the height of one hundred and sixty feet under the key-stone, and it is supported by four large pillars, each being thirty eight feet in circumference, and composed of thirty one columns, which are grouped together; above the arcades of the nave, there is a very narrow gallery. The edifice is lighted by one hundred and thirty windows.

There are amongst the stained glass windows, several which deserve to be, particularly noticed. I will here point out their places, after the work of E.-H. Langlois, on stained glass, and that of Gilbert on the Cathedral [1].

---

[1] *Historical description of the Cathedral of Rouen*, by Gilbert. Rouen, Ed. Frère, 1837, 8vo.

« Left aisle, in going up, opposite the fourth arcade of the nave : upper panes occupied by several subjects taken from the life of saint John the baptist, saint Nicolas, etc. We may remark curriers or tanners, and, near a sort of gallery supported by columns, a stone cutter and a sculptor making the capital of a column. A little farther up, we perceive a church supported by arches, in the construction of which, several masons are busily employed. Near it, is a woman kneelling, and holding up with both her hands the plan of a gothic window.

Same aisle, in going up, and opposite the fourth arcade of the nave : a window occupied with subjects relative to the life of saint Sever.

---

with 3 plates. — *Essay on ancient and modern painting on glass*, etc., by E. - H. Langlois. Rouen, Ed. Frère, 1832. 8vo, with 7 plates.

Left aisle of the choir, opposite the fourth arcade : a window entirely occupied with the life of saint Julian-the-hospitaller.

Same aisle, between the semi-circular lateral chapel and the chapel of the Virgin : two windows, representing the life of Joseph, the son of Jacob. We may still read, although with difficulty, the name of the painter and glazier. It is inscribed on a phylactery, in the following manner :

CLEMENS VITREARIUS CARNOTENSIS, M...

On the other side of the choir, between the chapel of the Virgin and the semi-circular lateral chapel : two windows, one representing the Passion ; the other the life of a saint. He is almost entirely represented naked from the head to the waist, and on horseback. Semi - circular chapel of the southern transept in the corner of the window, the martyrdom of saint Laurent. »

3

All these windows date from the end of
the XIIIth century. The most curious is
that representing the life of saint Julian-
the-hospitaller.

The Cathedral contains likewise several
fine specimens of windows of the time of the
renaissance. We must remark, especially,
those which represent the life of saintRomain,
in the chapel dedicated to that bishop and
those which decorate the chapel of saint
Stephen. We perceive, in the latter, saint
Thomas touching the wound of Jesus—
Christ; Christ preaching in the desert;
Christ appearing to Mary—Magdalen; etc.

The edifice is also lighted by three large
roses (circular windows); two at the extremities of the transept and the other above the
organ. Of these three windows the western
is by far the finest. In the centre of it, the
Eternal Father is represented as surrounded
by a multitude of angels having each different musical instruments, around it are ten

figures of angels, each holding an instru-
-ment of the Passion.

The present organ of the Cathedral is
a large sixteen feet one, and is placed
beneath the western circular window. It
was made by Lefevre, the celebrated organ
maker in Rouen, in 1760.

The choir is surrounded by fourteen pillars. Before 1430, its upper part was only
lighted by a small number of narrow windows. Since that time, it has been lighted
by the fifteen large windows, which we now
see. In 1467, under the cardinal d'Estouteville, the chapter caused stalls to be made,
which are very curiously sculptured.

A stone screen, of a style which harmo-
nized with the rest of the edifice formerly ornamented the entrance to the choir : In 1777,
it was replaced by the present. This screen,
notwithstanding its beauty, is unfortunately
not in a style correspondent with the rest
of the church. The upper gallery is sur-

mounted by a gilt figure of Christ, made of
lead, by Clodion. Between the pillars,
we remark two marble altars, each ornamented with a white marble statue. That
to the right is the statue of the Virgin, a
much esteemed sculpture by Lecomte. This
altar has retained the name *autel du vœu* (or
the altar of the vow) since 1637, on account of
a grand procession, which took place at that
time, to obtain the cessation of the plague.
The procession, in reentering the church
stopped before this altar, on which the ci-
vic authorities placed a silver lamp, weigh-
ing forty marks. The statue to the left is
that of saint Cecile, the patroness of musi-
cians. This sculpture is also from the chisel
of Clodion. Both altars are ornamented
with handsome bas-reliefs, the one to the
right representing, Jesus-Christ placed in
the tomb; that to the left, Saint Cecile, at
the moment of her death.

The actual existence of a library in the

Cathedral, may be traced back as far as the
year 1424. The canons, caused to be erected,
for that purpose, over the cellar of the chapter house, the large building which we see at
present. It was about one hundred feet long
by twenty five broad. They ascended to it
by a handsome gothic staircase, erected by
order of the cardinal William d'Estouteville,
during the second half of the XVth century,
and placed in the corner of the northen transept. This library was plundered and destroyed by the calvinists, in 1562, but, was
restored by the archbishop Francis de Harley.

In 1788, the chapter ordered an addi-
tional story to be built over the library,
destined to receive the records of the church.
The higher portion of the staircase which
conducts to this story, was erected in 1789,
and in the same style as the rest of it.

As far as 1112 the cathedral possessed
several manuscripts, which were destroyed
in the fire of 1200.

3.

A great portion of the books of the cathedral are now deposited in the public
library at the town-hall.

There are twenty five chapels in the circumference of the Cathedral. The most
spacious, and the first to the right on entering, is that of Saint-Stephen, *la grande
eglise*. It was formerly the *Parish church*
of Notre-Bame.

At the extremity of this aisle of the
nave in going up, is the chapel of *petit Saint-
Romain*, where the tomb of Rollo, the
first duke is situated. This prince had formerly been buried in the sanctuary, near
the great altar, which, at the time, was
situated at the higher end of the present
nave. The altar having been removed farther back, the remains of Rollo were deposited in the corner arcade where they
now are. Above the arcade is the following
inscription on a table of black marble, of
which the following is a translation.

Here lies Rollo, the first duke, the founder and father of Normandy, of which he was at first the terror and the scourge, but afterwards the restorer. Baptised in 912 by Francon, archbishop of Rouen, and died in 917 [*]. His remains had formerly been deposited in the ancient sanctuary, where is at present the upper end of the nave. The altar having been removed to another place, the remains of the prince were deposited here, by the blessed Maurille, archbishop of Rouen, in the year 1063.

On the opposite aisle, and exactly opposite the chapel we have just left, is that of Saint-Anne. The remains of Guillaume-Longue-Epée, the son and successor of Rollo, who was assassinated in an island of the Somme, by order of Arnould, count of Flanders, are deposited in this chapel. His remains are placed like those of his father, in an arched corner, above which, is the following inscription, which we translate thus.

[*] It is an error : Rollon did not die till the year 931 or 932.

Here lies Guillaume-Longue-Epée, son of Rollo, duke de Normandy, killed by treason in the year 944. His remains had formerly been deposited in the ancient sanctuary, where is at present the upper end of the nave. The altar having been removed to another place, the remains of the prince were deposited in this place by the blessed Maurille, in the year 1063.

What has become of those funeral monuments, erected formerly in the choir of the Cathedral, in honour of kings, princes or warriors? Who will assure us that the inscriptions placed at present in the sanctuary, point out to us, the illustrious dead whose tombs we seek? Where is the heart of Charles V[th], which was deposited in the middle of the sanctuary? That of Richard-Cœur-de-Lion, to the right of the high altar? The remains of Bedford, the son, the brother and the uncle of kings, of that Bedford, who, according to Pommeraye, was interred to the left of the high altar, and whose tomb stone they now shew us,

behind the altar, which tells us that he was
interred on the right side of it? Of all the
tombs which existed formerly in the choir of
the Cathedral, there remains but three
modern inscriptions on marble slabs, which
have been placed by chance. These three
inscriptions are those of Richard-Cœur-
de-Lion, Henry the Younger one of his
brothers and the duke of Bedford. On the
3oth of july 1838, being guided by historical traditions, they had the idea to
dig at the spot marked by the inscription to
Richard, and discovered the statue which
formerly decorated his tomb. This statue,
which is hewn out of a single block of very
fine free stone, has been deposited provisionally in the chapel of the Virgin. It is
six feet and a half long, and represents king
Richard in a recumbent posture, his head
supported by a square cushion, wearing
a crown enriched with precious stones;
his feet are supported by a crouching lion.

On his left hand was a sceptre of which
we only see the remains ; the right hand has
disappeared. The princes, mantle descends
nearly to his ancles, in wide folds. It is
over a tunic which reaches up to the neck,
and which is bound round the body, by an
embroidered belt of which the end hangs
in front below the knee. These searches
were continued on the 31st of july, and
the heart of Richard was found ; it was
enclosed in a double box of lead, and what
must leave no doubt of this precious disco-
very ; the following inscription in letters of
the time was engraved on the lid of the box :

HIC : JACET : COR : RICARDI : REGIS :

ANGLORUM :

The heart has been provisionally depo-
sited in a private press in the sacristy.
These researches were skilfully directed by
Mr Deville.

Let us now enter the chapel of the Virgin, and admire the treasure which it contains.

To the left on entering, is a monument of stone, without inscription or statue. It is that of Peter de Brezé, count of Maulevrier, grand senechal of Anjou, Poitou and Normandy. He was killed at the battle of Montlhery, the 16th july 1465. This monument is remarkable by its graceful proportions, its elegance and the delicacy of its architecture. It is composed of two pilasters of the arabesque style, supporting a pointed arcade, surmounted by a pediment; the whole of it is in open work and decorated on all sides with the initials P B, in gothic letters. The niche of the tomb is about five feet wide by about four deep. Its height is six feet four inches to the key of the vault, and decorated with a shield bearing the arms of the deceased. Before the revolution, the same sheild, decorated the three pannels of the base of the monument.

We may still perceive the trace of the des-
troyers chisel. The entire height of the
mausoleum is seventeen feet. The points of
the two pilasters rise two feet and a half or
three feet above the rest; which would make
the total height of the monument of about
twenty feet.

The name of Peter de Brezé, is honou-
rably mentioned in our annals at the time of
the conquest of Normandy. It was he who
received the capitulation of the castles of
Harcourt, Gisors, Chateau–Gaillard. It was
he, who first entered Rouen, when that
town opened its gates to Charles VIIth [1]. The
statue of Peter de Brézé and that of his
wife, Jeanne du Bec–Crespin, were formerly on the monument ; but they do not now
exist and no one knows when they have
been taken away.

---

[1] *Monuments of the cathedral of Rouen* , by A.
Deville. Rouen, N. Periaux, 1837, 8vo, with 12 plates.

Next to it, is the monument of Louis de
Brézé, grand-son of the latter, who died
in july 1531. The celebrated Diana of
Poitiers caused this mausoleum to be raised to his memory. The body of the monument is supported by four columns of black
marble, with capitals and bases of white
alabaster. Between these columns is a
coffin, on which the white marble statue of
the grand senechal, is laid. The deceased
is stretched on his back, his features are
convulsed : one may see that he has just
expired. The body is quite naked, the left
hand is laid on his breast. The cenotaph is
of black marble. The perfection of this
sculpture causes it to be attributed to the
celebrated Jean Goujon. Behind this statue,
there was formerly another of the same personage, he was represented in the dress of
a count, with the collar of Saint-Michael,
and a crown on his head. We now only
find the marks of the fixtures which fastened

4

it to the monument. At each end of the
recumbent figure, are two statues of women in
alabaster. Diana of Poitiers in the dress of
a widow, with her arms crossed, is kneeling
at the head. At the feet, is that of the
virgin holding the infant Jesus : it was
according to general opinion, of the time of
Pommeraye, who speaks of paintings,
figures, tapers and chaplets suspended round
the latter statue. There were two inscriptions, one in prose, the other in verse. Both
were erased at the revolution, but they
have been replaced since; the following is
a copy of the prose one :

Loys de Brezé, en son vivant cheualier de
l'ordre, premier Chambellan du Roy, grand Se-
neschal, Lieutenant-général et gouverneur pour
le dict Sieur, en ses pays et duché de Normendie,
Capitaine de cent gentilz hommes de la maison du
dict sieur et de cent hommes d'armes de ses ordon-
nances, Capitaine de Rouen et de Caen, Comte de
Mauléurier, Baron de Mauny et du Bec-Crespin,
Seigneur Chastellain de Nogent-le-Roy, Ennet,
Bréval et Monchauvet. Après avoir vescu par le

cours de nature en ce monde en vertu, jusques à l'âge de LXXII ans, la mort l'a faict mettre en ce tombeau pour retourner viure perpétuellement. Lequel décéda le dymence XXIIIe jour de juillet de mil v^{ce} trente ung. 1531.

A third inscription, which probably had not been perceived in 1793, is seen at the upper corner of the left side :

Hoc Lodoice tibi posuit Brezæe sepulchrum,
Pictonis amisso mæsta Diana viro.
Indivulsa tibi quondam et fidissima conjux,
Ut fuit in thalamo, sic erit in tumulo [1].

Some witty people have remarked that the duchess of Valentinois spoke truly, and that she was *as faithful* in one case as in the other.

Above the entablature, the equestrian

---

[1] O Louis de Brezé, Diana of Poitiers, afflicted by the death of her husband, has raised this monument to your memory, she was your inseparable companion, your very faithful spouse in the conjugal state, and will be equally so in the tomb.

statue, of the senechal, in white marble is
placed. On each side of the arcade, which
contains this statue, are four cariatides
crowned with flowers, and representing: the
two to the right, prudence and glory ; those
to the left, victory and faith. On the frieze,
under some figures bearing festoons, we find
this motto : *tant grate chevre que mal giste*.
The coping is an attic forming a niche, in
which is placed an alabaster statue ; it holds
a sword and represents power, according to
some, justice and prudence, according to
others.

In the frieze above the figure is the following inscription : *In virtute tabernaculum
ejus*. The cornice is terminated by two
goats supporting the armorials of the senechal. The whole of the frieze is of alabaster,
while the architrave and cornice are of black
marble. This mausoleum, which is one of
the most remarkable productions of the arts,
under Francis I[st], is attributed to Jean

Cousin, or to a sculptor not less celebrated, Jean Goujon.

The monument of the cardinals of Amboise, which is more splendid, but not of so pure a style, decorates the right side of the chapel : it is placed in the thickness of the wall. After working for seven years without interruption, it was at last completely finished in 1525, under the archbishop d'Amboise, the second of the name : we say archbishop, because at that time the prelate had not been invested with the roman purple. The bodies of these two cardinals are not deposited in this monument; they are interred in in a vault at the foot of it and which is only large enough to contain the two leaden coffins, which are supported on iron bars. The sepulchre was violated during the revolution, and the coffins carried off. On the lower part of the monument, are six beautiful little statues, in niches separated by pilasters, representing faith, charity, pru-

dence, power, justice and temperance. All
these statues are of white marble. On the
tomb, which is of black marble, the two cardinals George d'Amboise uncle and nephew
are placed. They are kneeling on cushions;
their heads uncovered and their hands
joined. The expression of prayer and piety
is perfect in the two figures, especially in
that of George d'Amboise I^st. At their feet
and on the front of the cenotaph, we find
the following inscription, in a single line,
which only concerns the cardinal-minister :

Pastor eram cleri, populi pater, aurea sese
Lilia subdebant quercus¹ et ipsa michi.
Mortuos en iaceo, morte extingvontvr honores;
At virtus, morte nescia, morte viret.

On the ground of the monument is a bas-
relief representing the patron of the two

---

¹ That is to say that the pope Julius IInd was of
the house of Rovere (*Quercus*).

prelates (saint George) overcoming the
dragon. On the sides, are eight different
figures, amongst which we discover the
virgin, several saints and more particularly
Saint-Romain, archbishop of Rouen during the first half of the VIIth century. A
voussure ornamented with sculptures, as
remarkable for their good taste as for the
richness of their ornaments, supports an
attic, where we find the statues of the
twelve apostles, two and two, in elegant
niches separated by pilasters.

These two monuments are not only remarkable by their magnificence and by the
recollections they awaken, they have another attraction, as an history of the art at
the time when the gothic style was giving
place to that of the renaissance.

These monuments were renewed in 1838,
in great perfection by M. Ubaudi, sculptor
of Paris.

The remains of cardinal Cambacérès, who

died at Rouen, on the 25th of october 1818,
are deposited in the little vault at the foot
of the monument of the cardinals of Amboise.

- The altar of this chapel is decorated with
a very fine picture by Philip de Champagne,
representing *the adoration of the shepherds*.
This picture is much esteemed by painters
and connoisseurs [1]. On the right, in leaving
the chapel of the virgin, is a monument
concerning which until recently, there were
only conjectures. It is the statue of a bishop
stretched on his back and under an arcade.
On the lower part of the sepulchre, are mu-

---

[1] The cathedral possesses also several other remarkable pictures; we distinguish amongst others, an
Annunciation, by Letellier of Rouen, nephew of
the celebrated Poussin: it is placed in the second
chapel of the left aisle, on entering by the great
portal. To the right and left of the choir, we find a
Samaritan, by Charles Tardieu, and *The lying in
the Sepulchre*, by Poisson.

tilated bas-reliefs, which one might suppose, were intended to represent a synod. At least, we may distinguish several personnages seated, holding books in their hands and a bishop in the midst of them as if presiding. On the upper part we remark angels bearing away the soul of the deceased, represented by the body of a young child.

M. A. Deville, in his work on *the monuments of the cathedral of Rouen,* has proved that this monument was that of Maurice, archbishop of Rouen, who died in 1235. I must not pass over the popular tradition, however ridiculous it may appear, which is attached to this monument. This tradition says, that the body of the personage laid under this stone, is that of a bishop who, in a fit of a passion, had killed his servant with the blow of a soup-ladle. The people add, that the bishop repenting, wished not to be interred in the church; but at the same time he forbad them to bury him

outside of it, and it was to obey this ambi-
guous order that they made him a tomb
in the thickness of the wall.

Not far from the chapel of the Virgin, in
the right aisle, on looking eastward, we
find the sacristy. We should stop a moment
before its stone partition with its iron door :
they are both much esteemed works of the
end of the XVth century. The partition wall
is from the liberality of Philip de la Rose,
chief-archdeacon, and was erected in the
year 1473 according to Farin, but 1479
according to Pommeraye [1].

Leaving now the inside of the cathedral
let us examine the exterior of this admirable edifice. Here, details are impossible; we must see the whole mass, to

---

[1] Mr Deville makes the dates between the years
1480 to 1482, according to the manuscript capitu-
lary registers of the cathedral.

form an idea of it. Who could number so
many pieces of sculpture, capitals, sculptured galleries, bas-reliefs, and ornaments,
which are multiplied under all forms? Historical explanations are those only which
can be offered to the reader. We may add,
that they are the most useful, since the rest
is an affair of the eyes. The whole of the
western facade, comprehended between the
two front towers, is from the munificence of
cardinal d'Amboise I. The building commenced on the 12th of june 1509, and
was finished in 1530. The bas-reliefs,
which decorate the doorways under the three
entrances from the porch, were more or less
mutilated by the calvinists in 1562. That on
the right is now scarcely to be recognized:
that of the great portal represents the gene-
alogical tree of Jesse, or of the family of the
Virgin; that on the left, the beheading of
John the Baptist; the latter porch suffered
considerably from a frightful storm, which

took place in 1683[1].

The tower, which terminates the facade to the north, bears the name of Saint-Romain. Its foundation is the most ancient part of the whole edifice; the rest was built later and at different periods. The whole was terminated in 1477, under the cardinal d'Estouteville. Before the revolution the tower of Saint-Romain contained eleven bells, there were four others in the pyramid, and only one in the Butter Tower, but which was heavier than all the others and of which I shall speak.

The tower, which terminates the facade to the south, is named the butter tower (*Tour de Beurre*), because, it was erected

---

[1] We perceive two counterforts, which have been lately erected on each side of the portal, under the direction of Mr Alavoine, to consolidate the front of the edifice, which had caused some fear, as to its solidity.

with the alms of the faithful, who, afterwards obtained leave to eat butter during
Lent : Its height is two hundred and thirty
feet. The first stone was laid in the month
of november 1485, by Robert de Croixmare, archbishop of Rouen. It was nearly
twenty two years in building, since the
edifice according to Pommeraye, was only
terminated in 1507. Before its completion, it was consecrated (in 1496), by
Henry Potin, suffragan to cardinal of Amboise I*.

On the 29th of september 1500, this cardinal gave 4000 livres, to be used in the
casting of a bell; wishing, that it might be
the finest in the kingdom. The furnaces were
already built at the foot of the tower; and
the mould commenced ; but, they remem-
bered that the wood work of the tower would
not be strong enough to bear such a colossus.
The mould was broken, and they made another which was smaller. The operation was

commenced on monday the 2nd of august
1501, at eight o'clock in the evening, after a
general procession round the Cathedral and
the archbishop's palace. The circumference
of this bell was thirty feet, its height ten feet
and it weighed 36ooo pounds. It is said, that
the founder, John le Machon, of Chartres,
who cast it, was so satisfied in having succeeded in this enterprise, that he died of joy
twenty six days after.

On the visit of Louis XVI to Rouen,
in 1786, the bell called George d'Amboise
was cracked. In 1793, it was converted
into cannons. Some pieces bearing the
following inscription were made into medals and are now very rare.

> MONUMENT DE VANITÉ
> DÉTRUIT POUR L'UTILITÉ
> L'AN DEUX DE L'ÉGALITÉ.
>
> ——
>
> MONUMENT OF VANITY
> DESTROYED FOR UTILITY
> THE SECOND YEAR OF EGALITY.

The door *of the librarians,* at the northern
extremity of the transept , has been named
so , from the booksellers shops formerly situated on each side of the court. Commenced
in 1280, this portal was only finished in 1478.
It was the usual entrance of great personnages, except the king and the princes of the
blood , who entered the church by the great
western porch. The bas-relief over the door
had never been finished : the two lower compartments are the only ones. The court,
which is before the porch of the librarians ,
was formerly a burying ground. They ceased
to inter, because a murder had been commit-
ted in it and it had not been purified. This
entrance to the church is ornamented with
an infinite number of bas-reliefs , some
representing subjects from the bible , others
extremely comical and even licentious ; several of these sculptures have of late been
cleaned to be moulded. To the left , when
facing the door , we perceive a man without

his head, negligently leaning on his elbow :
in his right hand a head is seen, which is
that of a pig.

If we wish to view the northern side, we
must enter the *sour de l'Albane* [1]. The col-
lateral chapels are lighted by nine windows,
which are surmounted by different ornaments. We also perceive, on some of the
lower windows of the tower of Saint-Romain,
the round arch of the XIth century; from
which one may conjecture that this portion
of the tower was spared from the conflagra-
tion, in the year 1200.

The porch of the *Calends*, was built at
the same period as that of the booksellers,
and is nearly disposed in the same manner.
Above the door, we distinguish a large bas-
relief, which is divided into three com-

---

[1] So called from the college of the same name
founded by Pierre de Colmieu, archbishop of
Rouen and cardinal of Albe.

partments: the lower one, says M*r* Gilbert, represents *Joseph sold by his brethren;* that in the middle; *the funeral of Jacob;* and the upper one *Jesus—Christ on the cross.* To the right and left of the porch, are several large statues, which are more or less mutilated, and a profusion of bas-reliefs, most of which represent the history of Joseph.

The facade of this porch, like that of the booksellers, is accompanied by two square towers of handsome proportions, and having large pointed windows.

On the tower which still exists in the centre, there was formerly a handsome pyramid of three hundred and ninety six feet in height, a monument of the talents of Robert Becquet and of the liberality of cardinal d'Amboise, the second of the name. It was commenced in the month of june 1542, and terminated in the month of august 1544.

This beautiful pyramid was destroyed by fire, on the 15*th* of september 1822; at seven

o'clock in the morning it had already fallen;
two hours after, the roof of the choir, that
of the transept and the third part of the roof
of the nave, had equally fallen in. The melted
lead of the roof was bought by M. Firmin
Didot and converted into types for printing.

We cannot give too many praises to the
zeal of M. de Vansay, prefect of the depar-
tment at that time : the misfortune hap-
pend on the 15ᵗʰ september, and already
on the 26ᵗʰ of the same month, the government having been informed and solicited
by that magistrate, ordered M. Alavoine,
one of the best architects, to go to Rouen,
and confer with the prefect on the means
of remedying the havoc caused by the
fire. Early in the year 1823, the roofs of
a aisles had already been repaired; and
a portion of the nave had been covered
with lead, by the 15ᵗʰ march of the same
year. The roofs of the choir and of the whole
transept, were also soon repaired; but,

for these parts, a copper covering was pre-
ferred as being more solid and less liable
to be destroyed. The raising and renewing
the lantern was terminated in 1829.

From this new platform, the pyramid
will rise majestically in the air, and of it we
already discover thirteen floors (the pyramid will be completed with one more),
each of four metres fifty centimetres, that
is to say a height of fifty eight metres,
or about one hundred and eighty feet. The
spire of the church was first erected of
stone but was overthrown by the electric
fluid, after that, it was twice built of
wood, and both times it became the prey
of the flames; to rebiuld it with wood would
have been gathering materials for a third
fire, but now it is made of cast iron and
in open work. At the summit of the spire,
there will be a small lantern surrounded by
a gallery for the purpose of meteorological
observations. The total weight of the

spire when completed, will be 600,000 kilogrammes, or about 1,200,000 pounds. It is composed of 2,540 pieces, not including 12,879 iron pins [1]. Lastly, this magnificent pyramid will reach an elevation of 436 feet; that is to say 40 feet higher than the former, and will only be 13 feet less than the highest pyramid of Egypt [2].

SAINT-OUEN.

The abbey of Saint-Ouen, is the most ancient, in Rouen and in the whole province of Normandy.

Founded in 533, during the reign of Clothaire I[st] and the episcopate of Flavius, the sixteenth archbishop of Rouen, (compre-

---

[1] The whole of these pieces of iron were cast at the foundery at Conches, a small town, which is situated at about twelve leagues from Rouen, and the expense is valued at 500,000 francs.

[2] For the description of the archbishop's palace, see the chapter on the civil monuments.

Saint - Ouen .

hending Saint-Nicaise), this abbey flourished particularly under the illustrious prelate, whose name it bears and who enriched it with his patrimony.

The 14ᵗʰ of may, in the year 841, the Normans landed at Rouen; the following day they burned the abbey of Saint-Ouen.

Rollo, having become a christian, and a peaceable possessor of Normandy, ordered the abbey to be repaired, and had the relics restored which the monks had carried off to secure them from the profanation of the Normans.

The monastery soon took the name of Saint-Oüen, instead of that of Saint-Peter, by which it was previously known.

The dukes Richard I and Richard II followed the example of Rollo, and continued the restoration of the abbey.

Such was the reputation of this monastery, that the emperor Otho, who had laid siege to the town during the reign of Richard Iˢᵗ,

surnamed *Sans-Peur,* demanded a safe con-
duct to come and perform his devotions at
Saint-Ouen.

Nicolas, son of Richard IIIrd, and the
fourth abbot under William the conqueror,
caused the edifice, which had subsisted until
then, to be demolished, and laid the first
stone of a new church in 1046. Nicolas died
too soon to complete the work; it was not
finished until the year 1226, by William
Ballot, the sixth abbot, who caused it to
be dedicated in the same year, on the 17th of
october, by Geoffroy, archbishop of Rouen.

The cloister and other buildings necessary for the use of the monks were finished
under Rainfroid, the seventh abbot; but,
in 1236, only ten years after the completion
of this church, the work of eighty years was
destroyed by fire in one day.

Through the liberality of the empress
Matilda and Henry IInd, her son, the monks
of Saint-Ouen succeeded in rebuilding their

monastery; but it was again completely destroyed by fire in 1248.

At last, the celebrated Jean (*John*) or *Roussel Marc d'argent*, the twenty-fourth abbot, was elected in 1303. Fifteen years later, he laid the first stone of the present magnificent church, which is so generally admired. In one and twenty years, during which the works of this edifice proceeded, the choir, the chapels, the pillars which support the tower, and the greater part of the transept were finished. These buildings cost 63,036 livres five sous tournois, or about 2,600,000 francs of the present money.

The edifice was not entirely completed until the beginning of the XVIth century; but, the tower existed before the end of the XVth. An english tourist [1] has expressed the following sentiments on this magnificent church:

[1] Dibdin's *Bibliographical*, *antiquarian and*

« You gaze, and are first struck with
its matchless window : call it rose, or
n arygold, as you please. I think, for delicacy and richness of ornament, this window
is perfectly unrivalled. There is a play of line
in the mullions, which, considering their
size and strength, may be pronounced quite
a master-piece of art. You approach, re-
gretting the neglected state of the lateral
towers, and enter, through the large and
completely-opened centre doors, the nave
of the abbey. It was towards sun-set when
we made our first entrance. The evening was
beautiful; and the variegated tints of sun-
beam, admitted through the stained glass of
the window, just noticed, were perfectly
enchanting. The window itself, as you look
upwards, or rather as you fix your eye upon

---

picturesque tour in France and Germany; London,
Payne and co. 1821, royal 8vo, vol. 1.

the centre of it, from the remote end of the abbey, or the Lady's chapel, was a perfect blaze of dazzling light : and nave, choir, and side aisles, seemed magically illumined. We declared instinctively that the abbey of Saint-Ouen could hardly have a rival ; certainly no superior. »

« The grand western entrance presents you with the most perfect view of the choir, a magical circle, or rather oval, flanked by lofty and clustered pillars, and free from the surrounding obstruction of screens, etc. Nothing more airy and more captivating of the kind can be imagined. The finish and delicacy of these pillars are quite surprising. Above, below, around, every thing is in the purest style of the XIVth and XVth centuries. On the whole, it is the absence of all obtrusive and unappropriate ornament which gives to the interior of this building that light, unencumbered, and faery-like effect which so peculiarly belongs to it, and which creates

a sensation that I never remember to have
felt within any other similar edifice. »

The length, within the walls, is four
hundred and sixteen feet eight inches (about
four hundred and fifty feet english measure),
which may be divided in the following
manner : The nave, two hundred and forty
four feet; the choir, one hundred and two
feet; the remaining portion, to the extremity
of the chapel of the Virgin, seventy feet eight
inches ; in the whole, eight feet eight inches
more than the Cathedral. The height under
the keystone is one hundred feet. The breadth, including the aisles, is seventy eight
feet; viz : thirty four feet for the nave, and
twenty two feet for each aisle. The transept
is one hundred and thirty feet in length,
by thirty four in width.

The church is lighted by one hundred
and twenty five windows placed in three
rows not including the three rosages. The
second row lights a circular inner gallery,

which is above the aisles, and several of
them offer paintings of great beauty.
Amongst others Saint-Romain is represented making himself master of the *Gargouille*, and forcing the Seine to return to
its bed.

Against the first pillar to the right, on
entering by the Western porch, is placed
a large marble vessel containing holy water.
By a very curious optical effect, we can
see the roof of the church in its entire
length.

The choir was formerly separated by a
magnificent screen, of which we find an
engraving in the *History of the Abbey*, by
Pommeraye. This screen was erected in
1462 by the munificence of the cardinal
d'Estouteville; in 1562, it was partly destroyed by the calvinists, and repaired in
1655, by William Cotterel, grand prior of
Saint-Ouen. This fine structure entirely
disappeared at the revolution.

Eleven chapels, including the one dedicated to the Virgin, surround the choir of the church. The first, in going towards the eastern extremity, contains the baptismal font, and is dedicated to Saint-Martial. There also, was formerly a very curious clock, which has disappeared within the last forty years. A small figure of Saint-Michael came out and struck the hours on a figure representing satan and then dissapeared.

In the second chapel, following the same direction, Alexander de Berneval, one of the architects of the church, was buried in 1440. He is represented, on the sepulchral stone which covers his remains, by the side of his pupil; the following inscription is engraved on this stone in gothic letters :

Ci gist maistre Alexandre de Berneval, maistre des Œuvres de Machonnerie du Roy, notre Sire, du baillage de Rouen et de cette Eglise, qui trespassa l'an de grace

mil ccccxl le vᵉ jour de janvier. Priez Dieu
pour l'ame de lui.

We also remark the statue of Sainte-Cécile,
which is placed between two pillars of the
corinthian order. The other chapels, except
that of the Virgin, do not offer any thing
remarkable.

English tourists will find in the latter,
the tomb of the youngest son of Talbot; the
following is the epitaph :

Ci gist noble homme Jean Tallebot, fils
du sieur de Tallebot, Mareschal de France,
qui deceda en annees de puerilite, le IV
Janvier MCCCCXXXVIII.

The interior of the church contains several fine paintings, such as : *The miracle of
the loaves*, by Daniel Hallé, and *a Visita-
tion*, by Deshayes, of Rouen, in the chapel
of the Virgin ; *an opening of the holy gate*,
by Léger, of Rouen, behind the pulpit on

the wall of the aisle. This painting has been much spoiled by the damp. The different chapels also contain some less worthy of notice.

The great tower is altogether a monument of great beauty. Its height is about one hundred feet above the roof of the church. It is surmounted by a crown wrought in open-work and of a fine effect. The total height of the tower is two hundred and forty four feet, from the pavement of the church. It is supported, in the interior of the edifice, by four pillars, each formed of a group of twenty four columns.

The whole body of the church is supported, to the exterior, by thirty fourarches, forming with the buttresses by which they are supported, a most magnificent ensemble.

The western porch from its unfinished state does not offer any thing remarkable except the rosace of which we have already spoken.

The southern porch, commonly called des *Marmouzets*, merits much more the attention of the curious, by the astonishing variety of sculptures, which ornament it. We may especially admire two pendants of a very bold execution.

Above the door, is a bas-relief, which is divided into three parts, representing the different circumstances of the sepulture of the Virgin, of her assumption and entrance into heaven. This porch is assuredly one of the most pure, light and perfect samples of gothic architecture. During the revolution, the church of Saint-Ouen was converted into a smithy. Afterwards they here celebrated the decadary feasts, promulgated laws, pronounced marriages, and even gave a great breakfast to the conscripts of the *year VII*, the first who went under that denomination. At last it was restored to its primitive use, the only one worthy of it, for we may say of Saint-Ouen : *Hic vere est domus Dei*.

The ancient abbey-house of Saint–Ouen was demolished, in 1816. So many historical recollections were attached to the existence of this edifice, that its loss is much regretted by the friends of the arts. This mansion was the ordinary place of abode of the kings of France, on their passage through this town. Henry II, Charles IX, Henri III, Henry IV, Lewis XIII successively inhabited it. Henry IVth, resided there four months; it was from this house that he addressed to the aldermen of his good town of Rouen those words which will never be forgotten :

Mes amis, soyez-moi bons sujets, et je vous serai bon roi, et le meilleur roi que vous ayez jamais eu.

In the public garden, formerly that of the monastery, and which lies to the north, east and south sides of the church, is a very curious construction, in the form of a tower, called the *Chambre aux Clercs*. It is without doubt a fragment of one of the churches,

Saint - Maclou.

which succeeded each other on this spot. It
is situated at the north-east angle of the northern transept. Its architecture is of the XIth
century. People have remarked, that it
holds as much resemblance to the remains
of a strong castle, as to a fragment of a religious edifice. The interior is divided into
two stories, the second contains the works
of the clock.

The meridian placed against the wall, to
the north of the basin, is that which ornamented the ancient exchange. On the lower
extremity of the obelisk, we remark a woman seated, representing Commerce. The
figure of Time points to the solar line. In
1815, the medallion of Lewis XVth was replaced, which had been taken away in 1792.
This monument is by Paul Slotds, a statuary
of the last century.

SAINT-MACLOU.

In the year 1228, this parish was situated

without the walls of the town. In that year,
Geoffroy de Capreville granted a portion of
ground belonging to himself, and situated
in the parish of Saint–Maclou, *without* the
town. At that time the church of Saint-Maclou was only a chapel, of which the con—
struction was not very remarkable. About
the middle of the XVth century, the erection
of the present edifice was commenced. In
the year 1511, the works were far advanced, the platform which was to support the
steeple having been already built.

This church was formerly called the *fille
aînée de Mg[r] l'archevêque.* The sacred oils
were kept in this church, and were distributed to the different parishes of the diocess.
This privilege was shown by two vases, supported on two iron bars on each side of the
cross, which surmounted the great porch.
In the general processions, the cross of Saint-
Maclou took precedence of all others, and
led the procession.

The church is one hundred and forty two feet in length, by seventy six feet in breadth, taking in the aisles. Its height, from the pavement of the nave to the extremity of the ancient steeple, was about two hundred and forty feet. This handsome steeple, in the form of a cone, rose to a height of one hundred and fifteen feet above the lantern : one could ascend to the cross, by the exterior of it, without a ladder. In 1705, it was shaken by a hurricane; thirty years later, it became dangerous : and they were obliged to take down the greater part of it. It was almost destroyed during the revolution, when its whole covering of lead was taken off, to make bullets. At present they are repairing the belfry which was erected instead of that steeple.

The interior of the church merits the whole attention of the curious. I will mention particularly the beautifully sculptured staircase, which leads to the organ. The

authors of *the picturesque and romantic tra-*
vels into ancient France, have not forgotten
to place this gothic jewel in their work.

The great porch of Saint-Maclou is very
remarkable. It had formerly three very com-
modious entrances; but, they have contri-
ved, at I do not know what time, to build
a house *before* and *quite close* to the south-
west door way; which, in consequence is
closed up.

The municipal administration lately decided that this house should be pulled down,
that the door which it closes up may be
opened; but it will be of no use but for the
general appearence of the front of the edifice,
as this door does not present, like the others,
any very interesting details of architecture.
It is more than probable that they existed
formerly, but, being hid from view, the door
was taken off and replaced by the plain one,
which exists at present; this loss must by
deeply felt, when we contemplate the sculp-

ture, which ornamented the other entrances and which strangers will not fail to admire, either in the western front or the northern porch from the rue Martainville. These sculptures, which are attributed to the celebrated Jean Goujon, consist principally of bas-reliefs representing different subjects from the Bible, such as *the death of the Virgin*, on the door in the rue Martainville; the *baptism of Jesus-Christ*, on the door of the great porch, etc. On the small door to the left, are also some very curious bas-reliefs.

Saint—Maclou still preserves almost the whole of its ancient painted glass windows, which are composed in general of isolated figures of saints, covered with canopies and in the style of the *Renaissance*. The lower portions of these paintings have been very much mutilated[1].

---

[1] The model in relief of this church and made in the first half of the xv[th] century, may be seen in the Museum of antiquities.

7

Almost opposite the northern porch of the
church, we find the entrance to what was
formerly the burying ground of Saint-Maclou, which answered the same purpose in
Rouen, as that of the SAINT-INNOCENTS, in
Paris. M. E.-H. Langlois has discovered, on
the columns of the buildings which surrounded this ancient churchyard, the fragments,
unfortunately almost shapeless, of a *macabre*
dance.

SAINT-PATRICE.

This church was built in 1535, on the
ground and in place of a smaller one. The
chapel of the passion, which is to the right
on entering the choir, dates from 1648, as
well as the side of the edifice, which faces the
rue Saint-Patrice. Quite near the church,
and in buildings belonging to the parish, a
community of priests had been founded in
1641, at the expense of the curate; they

had several privileges allowed by the king. They could enter fifteen *muids* of wine, without paying duty for it, they could take eight bushels of salt in the year, from the kings stores and at the merchant's price, and give the right of *committimus* to all ecclesiastics, after a year's residence in the town.

The church of Saint—Patrice, has some stained glass windows of the greatest beauty. They are of the XVIth century, which was the most brilliant period of painting on glass in France.

M[r] Langlois, in his excellent work, which I have already cited, gives a description of the painted glass windows. The whole interior of the chapel, which is situated at the extremity on the left side, and facing the east, is remarkable for the beauty of its windows. Most of them bear the date of their execution, and the name of the donor. The pulpit of Saint—Patrice was formerly

in the church of Saint-Lô ; it is of the style
of the *Renaissance*, and in good taste.

SAINTE-MADELEINE.

From the avenue of the Mont-Riboudet,
we perceive this elegant church at the end of
a row of young trees, It is built after the
plans of Lebrument and ornamented by the
chisel of Jadoulle ; this modern building is
distinguished by the beauty of its architecture and of its sculptures. It was terminated
and consecrated the 7th april 1781.

The front, which faces the south, is composed of a peristyle, supported by four corinthian columns. In the pediment, above
the entablature, we perceive a bas—relief,
which represents a *woman suckling children*,
the symbol of charity. The representation of
this virtue could not have been better placed, than on the front of a church adjoining
the Hôtel-Dieu.

The interior of the edifice is composed of a nave and two aisles, at the upper extremity of the nave rises an arched dome, which is surmounted on the outside by an obelisk supporting a globe.

Several costly pictures decorate the chapels. Those which are perceived at the extremities of the two aisles are more particularly esteemed. They are by Vincent, a distinguished painter of the french school. That on the right represents the *cure of the blind man ;* that on the left, the *cure of the paralytic.*

The chapel of the *religieuses* of the Hotel-Dieu, is situated behind the high altar.

(For a description of the hospital, see farther on, the article on civil monuments).

SAINT-SEVER.

In the commencement of the VIth century, Rouen possessed a bishop of this name. At

7.

first, it might be natural to think that this
bishop was the patron of the church of Saint-
Sever; but it is not so. The following
legend, is the history of this foundation,
in a few words.

In the reign of Richard Ist, third duke
of Normandy, two ecclesiastics of Rouen
made a pilgrimage to the sepulchre of Saint-
Sever, bishop of Avranches. The body of
the saint was deposited in the neighbourhood
of *Mont—Saint—Michel,* in a church surrounded by forests. A priest lived alone in the
neighbourhood. The two ecclesiastics, from
an excess of devotion resolved to carry away
the remains of the bishop. The priest heard
of it and put a stop to their enterprise. They
returned to Rouen, and humbly begged
Richard, whose consent they easily obtained to authorize the removal of the remains,
and in spite of the tears and remonstrances
of the inhabitants, they carried off the holy
relics, which they forwarded to Rouen. The

procession rested at the hamlet of Emendreville (now the suburb of Saint-Sever). Here
the miracle, which had already been shown
several times on the road, was renewed
again, that is to say, the shrine which contained the remains of the saint became so
heavy, that it was impossible to raise it,
until they had made a vow to build a chapel
on that spot; such is the origin of the
church of Saint-Sever. Till then this place
had been called Emendreville. It retained
that denomination about four centuries
afterwards; but at last it took the name of
the saint, in whose honour the parochial
church had been built. The present church
was consecrated on the 27ᵗʰ january 1538.
Neither its interior or exterior offer any
thing worthy of notice.

SAINT-ROMAIN.

This was the chapel of the ancient *Carmes
déchaussés*. Those fathers obtained letters

patent on the 27th july 1624. They purchased a house at the entrance of the suburb
Bouvreuil; which was then in the parish of
Saint-Godard, and laid the foundations of
their monastery. The duke of Longueville,
laid the first stone of their church on the
20th november 1643, which they demolished
in 1678, to build a new one, of which the
first stone was laid in the month of july
1679, by Mr Pierre de Bec–de–Lièvre, first
president of *the Cour des Aides*, who untill
the time of his death, which took place in
july 1685, paid the whole expenses of the
building. After his death, his two sons
MM. Pierre and Thomas–Charles de Bec–
de–Lièvre, finished the edifice at their own
expense. This is the present church : it was
consecrated on the 21st of december 1687.
In 1791, it was dedicated to Saint–Romain,
as one of the chapels of case of the town of
Rouen. After having been shut for a time,
it was again placed amongst the chapels

of ease, in 1802. It is now a parochial
church. On the front, which faces the east,
we find the following inscription in large
letters of gold :

SANCTO ROMANO

PATROCINANTE.

This church contains some extremely curious antiquities. The first, without doubt,
is the monument of the archbishop Saint-
Romain, which is of granite, and forms,
if I may say so, the high altar in the choir,
as the top of the high altar covers the monument, which is elsewhere very plainly seen.
It was formerly in the crypt of Saint-
Godard, where Saint-Romain was buried.
It was brought afterwards to this church on
the 20th february 1804. The ashes of the
illustrious prelate had been dispersed by the
calvinists, in 1562.

We may also admire the beautiful painted glass windows, which were brought

partly from Saint-Maur, Saint-Etienne-des-Tonnelliers, and Saint-Martin-sur-Renelle. The following is an explanation: In the first chapel, *a Transfiguration*, to the left on entering. In the next chapel *a holy Family*. This chapel contains also a beautiful small marble statue *of Saint-Louis*, and a bas-relief, by Jadoulle, representing *Tobit burying the dead*. The first chapel to the right, contains the font : there is a remarkable painted glass, divided into six partitions, which represents *the history of Adam*. It is in this chapel that we find a very curious cover of some baptismal-fonts, which was brought from the ancient church of Saint-Etienne. The bas-reliefs, which ornament it, represent *the Passion of Jesus-Christ*. In the sort of lantern, which surmounts the cover, is *a Resurrection*. These sculptures on wood, which are of great beauty, are of the begining of the XVIth century. At the farther end of the chapel, is a fresco painting by Pécheux representing *the baptism of Jesus-Christ.*

In the next chapel, which is dedicated to Saint-Theresa, we see *Sainte-Geneviève,* the patroness of Paris. In her left hand she holds a book, and in her right a lighted taper. Satan tries to blow it out with a pair of bellows, while, behind the saint, an angel is ready to light it again. These different painted glasses were brought from Saint-Maur.

In the chapel of Saint-Joseph, is a painted window representing *Saint-Stephen before his judges.* In the chapel of the Virgin, which is opposite, wee see *Saint-Stephen stoned;* these two painted windows belonged to the church of Saint-Etienne-des-Tonneliers.

Some glasses of the higher windows, brought from Saint-Martin-sur-Renelle, represent *the passion of our Lord.*

In the choir, in the chapel to the left,

Tobit burying the dead, above we see *the resurrection of Lazarus;* in the same window *Job on the dunghill;* and underneath, *the Lord's supper.*

In another chapel of the choir, opposite to the former, is *Jesus-Christ in the temple, overthrowing the tables of the money-changers;* beside it, is *the rich man at table;* Lazarus is at the outside of the door. The stained of these two chapels belonged to Saint-Maur. glass Most of them, from the richness of their coloring, and the perfection of their execution, are very remarkable.

Under the dome at the top of the nave, are five different fresco, paintings which represent different acts relative to the life of the patron of the church. One represents *the consecration of Saint-Romain as bishop:* in another, *he overthrows the pagan temples;* farther on, is *the miracle of the dragon or Gargouille;* next to it, is the procession of the shrine to obtain the deliverance of a

prisoner, a ceremony which was instituted after the miracle of which we have already spoken. *The apotheosis of Saint-
Romain* crowns these four paintings.

At the top of the sanctuary, behind the
high altar, there is also another fresco by
Pêcheux, *representing the agony of Jesus-
Christ*. The painting receives the light from
above, by an opening made expressly for
that purpose.

The organ, which was made by M^r Le-
breton, of Rouen, was received on the 11th
july 1830. It is composed of four keys,
forty two registers, and one pedal. Although
modern, the church of Saint-Romain, merits as we see, to be examind in all its details.

SAINT-GODARD.

The origin of Saint-Godard is unknown,
all that can be affirmed is that there existed anciently on this spot a chapel dedi-

8

cated to the Virgin. This latter circumstance induced the belief for a long time, that the first Cathedral was erected on this place. It will suffice, to establish the contrary, to say that the church of Saint-Godard, was included within the interior of the town only at the commencement of the XIIIth century.

In the year 533, and not 530 as Farin says, whose chronology is often erroneous, the archbishop saint Godard was interred in the subterraneous chapel of this church, which then changed its ancient name for that of the holy prelate, whose remains it had received. Saint-Romain was also interred in the same chapel.

It was only after different additions that the church of Saint-Godard became what we now see it. It is one hundred and fifteen feet long, by seventy eight broad. In 1556, its organ was a very small one; it was afterwards enlarged; but, in 1562, it was destroyed by the calvinists. The present organ, which was established in 1640, is the work of a scotchman, named George Lesselié.

The church of Saint-Godard, when suppressed at the second circumscription of the churches of Rouen, saw all its ornaments and riches pass to the parishes of Saint-Ouen and Saint-Patrice. Amongst the ornaments, we will mention its admirable painted windows, which were the finest in France, according to Farin and Levieil [1], whose opinion has become an authority. A great many of these glasses were broken in the *chambre aux clercs* of Saint-Ouen. When reopened for religious purposes, in 1806, the church of Saint-Godard became again possessed of two of its finest windows : that of the chapel of the Virgin, to the right facing the choir, and that of the chapel of Saint-Nicolas, on the opposite side. The first represents the

---

[1] *The art of painting on glass.* 1774, folio, fig.

mother of the saviour, and the kings of Judea from whom she was descended. The celestial head of the Virgin is of astonishing beauty of composition.

The window of the chapel dedicated to Saint-Nicolas represents differents acts of the life of saint Romain; and the painter, one may imagine, has not forgotten the history of the *Gargouille*. These two windows are each thirty two feet high by twelve in width. Nothing can be comparable to the beauty of the colour of these two windows; from thence came the proverb, in speaking of wine of a purple colour : *It is the colour of the windows of Saint-Godard.*

SAINT-NICAISE.

The church , that is to say, the primitive chapel which was built on this spot, was one of those which were founded , about the middle of the VIIth century, by the illustrious archbishop saint Ouen. It was at that time

very far out of the city, since the limits on
this side of the town extended only as far as
the streets de l'Aumône, and Robec, during
the life–time of saint Ouen. It was only six
hundred years after, under saint Louis, that
the church of Saint–Nicaise was comprehended within the interior of the town. The
choir of this church is remarkable for the
symmetry of its proportions. Its organ was
placed in 1634. The remainder of the architecture of this church does not offer any
thing to fix the attention. At the eastern
extremities of the aisles, we perceive two
mutilated painted glass windows; but
which nevertheless call forth the admiration
of the connaisseur. The one of them represents the three christian virtues, the other,
two figures of the same description, with
that of a bishop. The heads are very beautiful, and the draperies quite dazzling, from
their brilliant colours.

8.

SAINT-VINCENT.

This church was formerly called *Saint-Vincent-sur-Rive*, because it was situated on the bank of the river. The treasurers of Saint-Vincent had the salt measures in their keeping, they were deposited in a small tower at the entrance of the church, for that purpose. When the boats loaded with salt passed by the church, they had to give a certain quantity to the parish, which has been since replaced by an annual sum of 140 livres. Saint-Vincent, like most other catholic temples, was pillaged in 1562 by the calvinists.

Saint-Vincent is a handsome production of the *renaissance*. The architecture of the interior is light and gracious, if we except the ornaments, which are not in very good taste, and which have been fastened on the pillars of the choir, in the middle of the last century, after the designs of the architect De France.

The painted glases of this church are very remarkable. At the lower extremity of the right aisle in looking towards the choir, we perceive a pane of glass, a part of which is done on pasteboard by Albert-Durer, representing the virgin kneeling beside several of the apostles. The draperies of the former are in admirable gothic style; the heads of the others are also very fine.

In the northern aisle, that is to say, to the left on entering by the great porch, opposite the choir, we remark a window representing the history of saint John the baptist. The lower pannel represents the *Decapitation* of the saint, whose head they are carrying to Herod, who is seated at table with Herodias. In the next window, in going towards the eastern extremity, there is a view of the church of Saint-Ouen, but it is unfortunately broken. We can only now distinguish its tower.

In the chapel to the left of the choir, there

is a window representing the miracle attributed to Ferdinand, better known under
the name of saint Anthony of Padua, and
taken from the lives of the saints, by the
reverend father François Giry.

The interior of Saint-Vincent, and especially the southern aisle, still offers some
very fine painted windows which are unfortunately very much injured.

SAINT-VIVIEN.

This church has given its name to the
street in which it is situated It was formerly
but a chapel in the midst of meadows and
marshes. In the year 1209, it was situated without the town. It was formerly
low and dark; in 1636, the roof was raised
to a greater height. Before the year 1661,
the organ was placed in the left aisle : at
this period, it was placed in its present
situation. This church does not offer any

thing very remarkable, unless perhaps its lofty steeple, in the form of a sugar loaf.

●●

CHAPELS OF EASE.

—

SAINT-GERVAIS.

Saint – Gervais was perhaps after the virgin, the first person to whom an altar was erected in Rouen. Neither Pommeraye, Farin, Toussaint – Duplessis, nor several other modern writers, have spoken of the origin of this church; the following is a sketch of it.

In 386, saint Victrice, then archbishop of Rouen, received from Saint-Ambroise a box of relics, amongst which were the remains of Saint-Gervais. Saint-Victrice caused a church to be erected in which were to

be deposited those venerable remains. The
archbishop tells us that he worked with his
own hands, and that he even helped to carry
the stones on his shoulders. Should not the
temple where the remains of Saint-Gervais
had been deposited, have been named after
this martyr? Was it natural to give another
name? Certainly not; and we may conclude
therefore that the present church of Saint-
Gervais has been erected on the ground
where that formerly stood, which Saint-
Victrice had caused to be built; and which
afterwards was raised into an abbey, and is
at the present time a chapel of ease. The
church of Saint-Gervais suffered considerably during the religious contests : in the year
1591, it was almost destroyed. At that time
the royal army had taken possession of it and
had established a battery near to it, which
caused great havoc in the town of Rouen,
this army was commanded by the Marquis
de Villars, for the league.

Strangers should not forget to visit an
extremely curious ancient monument, the
crypt of Saint-Gervais. It is immediatly
under the choir of the church. The descent
is by a stair-case composed of twenty eight
stone steps. The length of this subter-
ranean chapel is thirty five feet, by sixteen
in breadth and fifteen in height. The two
first archbishops of Rouen, saint Mellon and
saint Avitien, are buried under the two arcades, which we perceive on the right and
left at the foot of the stair—case. These
arcades had been walled up at the time of
the religions troubles ; in 1723, they were
opened again. The monument of saint Mellon is that to the left on entering. We here
discover the only vestiges of roman architecture, which are to be found in this town.
The roman road, which existed sixteen centuries ago, between the ancient *Rothomagus*
and *Juliobona*, passed close to this church.

William the Conqueror, when mortally

wounded by the pummel of his saddle, on his way to Paris, caused himself to be carried to the priory of Saint-Gervais, where he died on the 9th of september 1087.

SAINT-HILAIRE.

In the year 1562, the calvinists entered by force into the town of Rouen, by the suburb of Saint-Hilaire, and destroyed at the same time the church of that name. It was rebuilt twenty eight or thirty years after. Like the church of Saint-Vivien, it has given its name to the quarter in which it is situated; and like it also, offers nothing worthy the attention of the antiquary.

SAINT-PAUL.

Farin and some other authors have said that this had been an ancient temple of *Adonis;* nothing however proves, or justifies such an assertion; and we only see in this, a popular tradition on which ,we must not rely.

Formerly this little church was very curious in some of its portions. It is the only one in Rouen, which offers the three semicircular *absides*, which we find in most of the monuments of the XIth century. The middle is the highest and projects farther out than the other two. There is a row of curious figures on the outside of the edifice in its whole circumference : some of which are represented with great moustaches. According to M[r] Cotman, who has remarked figures of a similar description in different parts of Normandy, these great moustaches must at first have been a satire upon the Saxons who wore them, when at the same time the Normans had their heads completely shaved. Robert Wace tells us that at the battle of Hastings the English took the Normans for an army of priests.

9

In the interior of the edifice, the triple
choir was separated from the nave by a semi-
circular arcade, the capital of which was
covered with sculptures, which have been
unfortunately destroyed. This nave was
modern, and dated only from the commencement of the XVIIth century, the most
ancient portion is from the commencement
of the XIth century.

The modern portion was destroyed some
years since. A new church in the form of
an ancient basilica has been erected close to
it, from the designs of M[r] Du Boullay. An-
tiquaries will learn with pleasure that the
administration of the town has taken measures to preserve the three *absides* of the ancient little edifice, with the intention of
using it as a sacristy to the new church.

The walk, at the extremity of which the
church of Saint-Paul is situated, was
formed in 1692 and 1693; but was only
the planted in 1729. The whole space from

watering place to the foot of mount Saint-Catherine was formerly a vast meadow with a few gardens. The road when finished was called the *Chemin neuf;* it is now called the *cours Dauphin*, so named in memory of the birth of the dauphin, son of Lewis XV.th.

At the extremity of this avenue there are several springs of mineral waters. They are called the waters of Saint-Paul, from the name of the parish. There are also several of similar description in the quarter Martainville, called la Marequerie.

●●●

PROTESTANT WORSHIP.

—

SAINT-ÉLOI.

Before the Seine was enclosed in its present bed, the church of Saint-Eloi was situated on an Island. Afterwards, without

changing place, it found itself situated on
the *terres neuves*, like the other churches,
Saint–Etienne–des–Tonneliers, Saint–
Clément, and Saint–Martin–du–Pont. In
1030, under the duke Robert, those new
lands were considered as suburbs of Rouen :
In suburbio Rotomagensi ecclesiam sancti
Eligii, etc.

The church of Saint–Eloi was formerly
considered as one of the best lighted in the
town of Rouen. There were, a short time
since, but are now walled up, three windows,
of which the painted glass was executed in the
XVIth century ; they have been transferred
to Saint–Mary's, to ornament the museum of
antiquities. Formerly there was a well in
the choir, but which is now filled up, from
which the water was drawn up by a chain,
from whence the proverb, still used in
Rouen, is derived : « It is cold as the chain
of the well of Saint–Eloi. »

This church has been granted for pro–

testant worship, since 1803. The number of persons who profess this worship in Rouen, is about 2,000. The service commences at eleven o'clock in the morning. English service is also performed in this church at three o'clock in the afternoon.

The *place Saint-Eloi* does not offer any thing worthy of notice; it was the ancient burying ground of the parish of that name : and has since become the poultry and game market.

●●

CHURCHES CLOSED IN 1791,

WHICH DESERVE THE ATTENTION OF THE ANTIQUARY.

———————

SAINT-PIERRE-DU-CHATEL,

At the top of the rue Nationale.

This religious edifice, which is of the

9.

XVth century, did not offer any thing remarkable but its tower, which is entire.

SAINT-ANDRÉ-DANS-LA-VILLE,

Rue aux Ours, near the rue de la Vicomté, was erected between the years 1526
and 1557.

SAINT-ÉTIENNE-DES-TONNELIERS,

At the corner of the street of that name,
and the rue des Iroquois.

The construction of this edifice, dates
from the commencement of the XVIth century.

SAINT-PIERRE-L'HONORÉ,

Rue des Bons-Enfans, at the corner of
the rue Ecuyère.

SAINTE-CROIX,

Rue Sainte-Croix-des-Pelletiers, at the
top of the street.

SAINT-SÉPULCHRE,

At the corner of the sreets Saint-George and de la Vicomté.

SAINT-LAURENT,

In the street of that name. Its tower merits principally the attention of the traveller ; it was commenced in 1490, and finished in 1501. The screen of Saint-Laurent was considered a chef-d'œuvre of architecture.

●●●

CIVIL MONUMENTS.

HÔTEL-DE-VILLE (TOWN-HALL).

The modern building which stands near the northern transept of the church of Saint-Ouen was the dormitory of the monks. It is now the town hall. The offices occupy the ground and first floor, the library and gallery of paintings the second. The great stair-case is remarkable for its elegance and lightness; it has been compared to that at Somerset house. On the first landing we find in a niche, the statue of Lewis XVth in his youth, from the chisel of Lemoine. The great stair-case, next the church, constructed from the designs of Le-

brument, the architect of the Madeleine, is
distinguished by the boldness of its architecture; it leads to the [library and gallery of
paintings. The new facade of the town
hall is composed of two wings which are
parallel at their extremities, and a peristyle
betwen the two former, but which does
not so far project. Two columns of the
corinthian order support the pediment, on
which the armorial bearings of the town
are sculptured; they are supported on one
side by Mercury and the attributes of Commerce, and on the other by Industry in
the likeness of Minerva. On the first floor
of the southern wing, there is a very
fine room, which is used for the meetings
of the municipal body; one of the rooms on
the second floor has been devoted to the
meetings of the royal academy, their former
room having been joined to the public library.

The ancient town-hall, which was built in

the year 1608, was situated at the corner
of the rue Thouret and the rue de la
Grosse-Horloge, and near the tower of the
belfry; the only portion of this building
which remains, is that which faces the rue
Thouret. This edifice having fallen into
ruin, it was decided that a new town-hall
should be erected. In 1757, a plan was
adopted, and the monument was to be raised
at the western extremity of the old market
place; but after having laid out one million
of francs, on the foundations alone, they
became terrified at the enormous sum, which
it would require. The municipal administration still possesses the model in relief of
the said monument : it was of very curious
architecture and may still be seen at the
Museum.

ARCHIEPISCOPAL PALACE.

This edifice adjoins the Cathedral church.
The principal body of the building, which

faces the street, was begun and partly finished in 1461, by the cardinal d'Estouteville;
but death overtook this prelate before he
had completed the whole. It does not appear
that his successor, Robert de Croixmare,
continued the works. It was, according to
Farin, the cardinal George d'Amboise I[st],
who terminated the edifice. The only remarkable portion of the interior of this edifice is that named the *gallery of the states*.
It is decorated with four large paintings by
Robert. They represent views of Havre,
Dieppe, Rouen and Gaillon, the once celebrated chateau of the archbishops of Rouen,
and built by the cardinal d'Amboise I[st], with
the savings which he made from his salary,
from the profits of his legation, and from
the large fines which he levied, with the
knowledge of the king, on the rebel towns
of Italy.

In 1508, when Lewis XIIth with his
queen came to Rouen, he alighted at the ar-

chiepiscopal palace. The dauphin Francis
of Valois, son of Francis I⁺⁺, inhabited it
also in 1531.

The modern building which looks on the
garden, and which is to the right on entering,
was erected at the commencement of the last
century. The library, which is appropriated
to the chapter of the cathedral, is situated on
the first floor.

PALACE OF JUSTICE.

When we say that the Palais-de-Justice
was erected by Lewis XII⁺⁺, in 1499, as a
court of exchecquer, which that prince had
arranged should be held at Rouen, we
must not comprehend that part of the
building called the *salle des Procureurs*,
or attorneys hall, which dates from 1493,
and which was erected (as we have mentioned at the article exchange), as a place
of meeting for the merchants of the town.
Even at the present time, this hall calls

Palais de Justice.

forth the admiration of the best architects.
Its length is one hundred and fifty feet, by
fifty in breadth. Its lofty roof is not supported by a single pillar; the ingenuity of
the work is here contrasted with its boldness
of conception. The only ornaments which
decorate the walls of the hall are elegant
empty niches, which are detached in relief,
and at equal distances. The principal staircase, which leads up to the salle des Procureurs, was erected a few years since, under
the superintendance of M. Gregoire. The
Conciergerie and prisons are situated under
this hall.

The Palais-de-Justice, properly so called,
forms as it were one side of a square, at the
northern extremity of the salle des Procureurs. Its facade, which looks towards the
south, is two hundred feet in length, and is
ornamented with every thing that the architecture of the time possessed of the richest
and most delicate. The angular pillars o

10

the piers are covered with canopied statues
and small steeples, which extend from the
base to the summit; the numerous ornaments, which surround the windows, those
which accompany and surmount the windows of the roof; the leaden balustrade
which surrounds the roof, the arcades
which form a gallery, and are carried along
the whole of the entablature, lasty, the
elegant octangular turret which occupies
the middle of the facade and separates it
into two equal parts, are of the greatest
beauty and purity of taste, in spite of a
certain mixture in the style, which charac-
terizes the transition from gothic architecture to that of the *renaissance*, style which
already began to be in use. The name of the
architect, unknown till recently, is Roger
Ango.

At the farther end of the salle des Procureurs is a door, which leads into the ancient *Grand'Chambre* (great Chamber), i n

which the court of assizes are now held.
This hall may be considered as the finest in
the kingdom. The ceiling, which is divided
into sculptured compartments, decorated
with gilt bronze ornaments, is of oak to
which time has given the appearance of
ebony. The whole of the flooring was formerly covered with *arabesques*, according
to the custom of the reign of Lewis the
XIIth. From this floor, an ancient fire place
which existed in the *Chambre de Conseil*,
or Counsel Hall, a curious painting which
the antiquarian Millin mentions in his *national antiquities* and on which witnesses were
sworn have all disappeared.

On the exterior, only two parts of this
elegant edifice, that which is exposed to the
setting sun, and the middle one to the south,
have retained their primitive beauty. The
latter is now under repair and renovation. At
the commencement of the last century, the
modern portion of the building which faces the

west, was erected. The front of this building
fell to the ground on the 10th of april 1812,
and brought down with it the whole ceiling,
which was painted by the celebrated Jouvenet, who, having his right hand paralysed,
painted with his left, and in a manner worthy
of such a painter, the *Triumph of Justice.*

Considerable embellishments have taken
place in the court of the Palais. The mas-
sive flight of stone steps, which led to the
salle des Procureurs, and which especially
hid from view the beautiful angular turret, has been removed. A new staircase has
been erected at the middle of the facade,
before the door of the prisons, the entrance
to which, is at the side. This staircase is
composed of a single straight flight, of five
metres (fifteen feet) in breadth, and is crowned by a porch in the style of the building.
The ancient wall, which closed the court on
the side of the rue aux Juifs, has been replaced by a cast iron railing, in the gothic

style. The front of the Palais being thus exposed to view, the aspect of the edifice becomes as imposing as picturesque. Behind the Palais-de-Justice, in the rue Saint-Lô, is a large building, which answers the purpose of a court of appeals, for the *cour royale*. The offices of the town-hall were established here during the revolution. It was formerly the residence of the first presidents of the parliament of Normandy.

TOWER DE LA GROSSE-HORLOGE.

The following inscription, which is engraved on a brass plate, and is perfectly well preserved, is placed above the door at the foot of the staircase.

En lan de lincarnacion nre segnour. mil ccc. iiii. et neuf. fu comencé cest berfroy : et Es ans ensuiues iusques en lan mil. ccc. iiii. et xviii. fu fait et parfait. ou quel. temps noble home mess. Guille de Bellen-

10.

gues cheuallier chambellen du Roy nostre
Sire estoit cappitaine de ceste ville. hono-
rable home pourueu et sage Johan de la
tuille bailly. et sire Guillaume alorge. Johan
mustel. Guille de gaugy. Richart de som-
mery. Nicolas le roux. Gaultier campion,
conseillers de la dicte ville. et pierres hermes
reseueur d'icelle.

Proceeding on , we ascend the tower of
the belfry , by a flight of two hundred steps,
at the top of which is the bell , with the following inscription :

✝ JE SUI : NOMME : ROUUEL : ROGIER :
LE FERON : ME FIST : FERE : JEHAN :
DAMIENS : ME FIST ✝

We perceive by this inscription , that this
bell was named *Rouvel*, and not *Rembol*,
as tradition would have it ; but it is better known under the name of the Cloche
d'argent (silver bell), although not a grain

of silver entered into the composition of it. It rings every night at nine o'clock. It also rings peals on occasion of any national rejoicings or public calamities. This bell was made in the year 1447; it was then called the *horloge du Beffroi*. The stone vault, which crosses the street, at the place still called *porte Massacre* (the murder gate) was erected in 1527. On each side of this arcade, we perceive the dial plates and medallions.

Under the Vault, in the centre, we see sculptures representing a shepherd tending sheep. On each of the sides, are other sheep grazing. To the left, and facing the old market place, we may read the following inscription : *Animam suam ponit pro ovibus suis*, which indicates sufficiently the allegory of this composition, if we did not also see on the opposite side these other words: *Pastor bonus*.

Beside the arcade, but nearer to the rue

des Vergetiers, the tower of the Belfry
rises. We perceive a platform at the top of
the tower, surrounded by an iron railing,
from whence is a view of the whole town.
Above is a dome, surmounted by a small
steeple.

THE COVERED MARKETS.

About the middle of the Xth century, Richard Ist, surnamed *Sans-Peur*, and third
duke of Normandy, caused a palace to be
erected on the Seine, which consisted of a
large tower and served at the same time as
a defence to the town. It was also the state
prison. Henry Ist added several buildings.
Several fortifications had been previously
erected, the former being then called the
Vieille-Tour (old Tower). This tower was
destroyed by Philip-Augustus; it was there,
according to the greater number of historians, that in 1204 the cruel John-Sans-

Terre caused his nephew, Arthur of Britanny, to be confined, and murdered him with his own hand. The present *halles* (covered markets) occupy the greater portion of the site formerly occupied by the palace and the *Vieille-Tour*, which has left its name to the two markets we are presently going to speak of.

Those vast warehouses for different manufactures, called *halles* (or marts), were erected in the second half of the XIIIth century, about the time when Lewis IXth fixed the fifth enclosure of the town of Rouen. These marts are considered the most important in France. The most considerable portion, and also the most ancient of the whole building, is set apart for the sale of linen cloths. Its length is two hundred and seventy two feet, by fifty in breadth. The roof is supported by two rows of stone pillars. The two other marts, one for coton stuffs and the other for worsted stuffs and cloth, are each two

hundred feet in length. These marts were
open till about the year 1493, at which time
they were enclosed, to prevent vagabonds
taking shelter in them. The linen mart separates the market which is held on this place in
to two unequal portions. The larger occupies
the north side, and is called the *place de
la Haute-Vieille-Tour;* it is reserved for the
sale of old linen, old utensils and particularly for the sale of crockery and glass ware.
The second occupies the south side, and is
called the Basse-Vieille-Tour, because it is
considerably lower than the other portion.
Several kinds of eatables are sold here, especially fish.

There formerly existed a every beautiful
fountain in the middle of the higher place,
which was composed of a triangular pyramid, surmounted by a statue of Alexander;
but not the least vestige of it remains. The
present fountain is supplied with water from
the Gaalor spring.

Near the linen-mart, we observe a remarkable edifice, which projects from the rest of the building, called the monument of Saint-Romain. This structure however does not form part of the marts, to which it has not the least resemblance. Neither did it form a part, of the palace of the ancient dukes of Normandy, as some persons still believe. The style of its architecture sufficiently indicates the time of its erection, namely 1542. The corinthian order of architecture appears in the whole height of the building. It was on the first floor that the celebrated old ceremony, called the *levée de la Fierte*, for the delivrance of a prisoner, took place every year [1].

In the neighbourhood of the linen and

---

[1] To have all accounts of this ceremony, see the work of Mr Floquet, entitled : *Histoire du Privilége de Saint-Romain*, etc. — Rouen, E. Le Grand, 1833, 2 vol. 8vo.

cotton marts , is the corn mart ; it is three
hundred feet in length, its breadth being in
proportion. It is open three days in the
week : mondays, wednesdays and fridays :
the two others marts are open only on fridays.

THE EXCHANGE.

Untill the year 1493, the merchants of
Rouen had no place of meeting alloted to
transact their commercial affairs. They met
however, in the cathedral but, without au-
thorisation. The municipal authorities, wishing to put a stop to this state of things ,
made an arrangement with the bailiff of
Rouen, who issued a decree : « That there
should be erected at the lower end of the
New—Market place, and at the expense of
the town , a large stone building, and on
the second floor of this edifice , a large hall
was to be reserved for the use of the merchants of the town , those of other nations

also having the same right, to meet and transact their affairs; which hall is to be named, for the future, the common town hall.»

The stone building here spoken of, is that vast wing, which closes the court of the *Palais-de-Justice* to the west; and the common town hall is that known under the name of *Salle des Procureurs* or *des Pas-Perdus.*

About the year 1664, the merchants company obtained a portion of ground on the quay, where they met untill 1827. Since then, that portion of ground has been given up to enlarge the quay. The meridian which ornamented this ancient exchange, is now placed in the garden of the town hall. Since the straightening of the quay, the uncovered exchange has been placed before the *Consuls* (or covered exchange) so that the one might communicate with the other : it occupies the portion of ground, which is situated between the rue Nationale and the

11

rue des Iroquois , and is surrounded by an
iron railing.

TRIBUNAL OF COMMERCE ,

COMMONLY NAMED THE CONSULS.

It is in the gallery on the ground floor ,
that the merchants meet , when the rainy
weather does not permit their meeting in
the uncovered exchange: This was formerly
the *Juridiction consulaire;* so its destination
has not been changed since the tribunal of
commerce is established here. In the middle
of the gallery on the ground floor, and to
the right on entering from the quay, we
remark a handsome staircase , which is
formed by a double flight of steps, from the
first landing. Before the revolution , the statue of Louis XVth was placed here.

This staircase leads up to the audience
hall of the chamber of commerce, which is
the most remarkable of the three rooms

which compose the first floor of the building. It is ornamented with a fine picture of Christ by Van Dyck. In one of the neighbouring rooms are two paintings of large dimensions, by Lemonnier, a native of Rouen. One of these paintings represents the audience given by Louis XVIth to the Chamber of commerce of Rouen, on the 28th june 1786, in the great hall of the archbishop's palace, called the *Salle des États*. All the figures are of natural size, and are striking likenesses. The subject of the other painting is allegorical.

There are three different entrances to this edifice, one from the rue Nationale, another from the rue des Charrettes and a third from the Quay.

THE CUSTOM-HOUSE.

The edifice containing the ancient custom-house being a great deal too small and incon-

venient for that purpose, it became indispensable to erect another building. For
this object, the municipal administration
opened a public competition on the 14th
october 1833, for the erection of another
edifice. In the month of may 1834, the
preference was given to the plan of M^r Ed.
Isabelle, a distinguished architect in Paris,
who was charged with putting his plan into
execution. The excavations were commenced on the 17th february 1835, in the presence of the mayor, the municipal council,
etc., and the building was terminated
in 1838.

The architectural appearance of this edifice reminds us a little of the severe style
of the florentine architecture; the large door-
way *is* ornamented with the attributes of
commerce, as likewise the coping of the
edifice; two bas-reliefs, of eight and a half
feet high, and sculptured on stone by David, representing the *symbols of navigation*

and commerce, decorate the middle of the
facade on the first floor. This building is
situated on the *Havre quay,* a little farther
on than the old one. It has three entrances :
the principal , on the quay, leads into
a large rectangular court, which is covered
with a cupola of cast-iron; opposite to the
entrance of this court, is placed against
the wall the fine bas-relief, which ornamented the front of the old custom-house , a very
handsome piece of workmanship by Coustou,
a statuary of the XVIIIth century ; it represents Mercury with the different attributes of
commerce. Two other entrances from the
quay lead to the offices and dwellings of some
higher persons attached to the customs.
The lateral entrances serve as outlets to
merchandise after having been searched or
examined in the covered court.

The bonded and examining warehouses
are on the ground floor, as likewise the
offices of the comptroller, sub-comptroller

11.

and searchers; the entresole is destined for
other offices; the first floor is occupied
with the dwelling and offices of the director;
and lastly, the second story contains the
dwelling of the principal receiver and the
residing comptroller.

The entrepôt réel, is situated, behind the
new custom-house; this warehouse is used
for warehousing merchandise after the duties have been paid. The front of this edifice which is situated in the rue des Charrettes, was erected in 1826.

PUBLIC SLAUGTERHOUSE.

Rue de Sotteville, suburb of Saint-Sever.

For a long time the municipal council
had occupied themselves with the idea of
endowing the town with an establishment of
this description, the want of which was im-
periously felt; numerous plans were presented and discussed; at last, after a thorough

examination, the town obtained, by royal
ordinance of the 18th august 1833, the au-
thorisation to establish a public and common
slaughterhouse, with apparatus for melting
the tallow, scalding house and tripe house,
on the fine property, which is situated in the
rue de Sotteville, at the corner of the *avenue
de Grammont*, bought for that purpose from
Mr Burel.

A public competition was opened at the
end of the year 1838 for the plans of this
establishment, and the prize was decreed,
on the 20th march 1834, to *Mr Etienne-
Théodore Dommiey*, an architect from Paris.

The first stone of this establishment was
laid by Mr H^y Barbet, the mayor of Rouen,
on the 28th july 1835, in the presence of
the civil and military authorities and a large
number of spectators.

This important establishment, which was
built within the period of two years, and
which is now completed, is one of the finest

of this description. The expences, including the purchase of the ground, amounted
to the sum of 970,000 francs, and the annual
product is istimated about 80,000 francs.

The principal entrance is from the *rue de
Sotteville*, a handsome gateway between two
gate houses gives a view of the whole
building. The total superficies of the buildings is of seven thousand three hundred
and thirty seven metres, or about the same
number of yards.

Spacious streets and avenues planted with
trees permit of a free access to all parts of
the establishment. It is well supplied with
water, and has a canal to carry off the dirty
water of the establishment, which allows
its being kept very clean.

To visit the slaughterhouse, apply to the
sceretary general's office at the town hall.

ROYAL COLLEGE,

Rue du Grand-Maulevrier.

The entrance court, is almost square, and surrounded on the four sides by buildings of a regular architecture. This portion formed the ancient college of the Jesuits. At a short distance to the north, and on a raised portion of ground, stands a large building formerly called the *Joyeuse seminary,* from the name of its founder, the cardinal de Joyeuse. These two establishments have now been united. That part, named *Joyeuse,* is exclusively reserved for the youngest children : they have their separate play ground, which is formed of the terraces of the garden. The courts, which are alloted to the other classes, are situated lower than the former. The college contains about two hundred boarders and five hundred day scholars.

The college church particularly deserves to be mentioned. Its porch is situated in the rue Bourg-L'abbé; we remark on the right of the entrance a statue of Charlemagne, which we recognise by the globe he holds in his hand; on the left, is that of Saint-Louis. The erection of this church was commenced in 1614. It was formerly intended to be attached to the college of the Jesuits. Marie de Medicis laid the first stone of this church, which was only finished in 1704, and dedicated on the 21ˢᵗ of december of the same year. Several paintings decorate the interior, which is grand and majestic. The public are admitted into this church during the hours of divine service.

The municipal administration has caused a handsome marble mausoleum to be erected to the memory of the cardinal de Joyeuse, the founder of the seminary, in one of the lateral chapels to the left on entering.

~~~~~~

HOSPITALS.

—

HÔTEL-DIEU,

*Rue de Lecat, at the extremity of the rue
de Crosne.*

The establishment of vast hospitals is very
ancient in Rouen. The one of which I am
speaking was formerly situated near the
cathedral, between the *Calende square* and
the *rue de la Madeleine.* The house which is
opposite the southern porch of Notre-Dame,
is a part of the remains of that hospital. In
1758, it was transferred to the new building,
which had been erected in 1749, on the
place called *the Lieu-de-Santé*, other buildings having been afterwards added.

The Hôtel-Dieu is exclusively reserved for the reception of the inhabitants of the town, excepting cases of urgency, which after having been treated during six months, are dismissed as incurable, and are admitted into the Hospice–Général, if they have dwelt during ten years in the town. More than four thousand persons are admitted into this hospital annually. About two thirds of the sick are under the care of the physicians, the remainder under that of the surgeons of the establishment. Different rooms are reserved for different maladies. One of these is alloted to soldiers; another, which is known under the name of *Gésine*, is reserved for lying in women. There is also a separate room for Children under five years of age, and several rooms for boarders.

There are in all fifteen rooms, containing together more than six hundred beds, the half of which are of iron.

The medical practice is divided into two

distincts parts; that of physicians, that of surgeons. Their visits are made regularly twice in the day.

The Hotel-Dieu, is at the western extremity of the *rue de Crosne-hors-Ville*, which is planted with trees, and offers a fine avenue. The buildings which form the hospital (properly so called), are those which are situated opposite the entrance gate which gives admittance to the vast court of the hospital.

The two hospitals are under the same superintendance which is renewed by one fifth, every year. This commission acquires each day a greater right to public gratitude and especially to that of the poor.

HOSPICE-GÉNÉRAL.

This hospital is situated in the lower part of the town, to the south-east, and occupies a vast portion of ground adjoining

12

the boulevard Martainville. Gratitude causes us here to mention the name of Claude
Groulard, first president of the parliament
of Rouen, in 1602: From that date the establishment of an hospital, really took place
for the reception of the poor sick inhabitants.
Previously, there existed only a subsidy, for
the relief of the poor. After Groulard, a
counsellor of parliament, named Damiens,
wishing to uphold more effectually the existence of the hospital, quitted his house and
situation, on purpose to live within and in
this way be nearer to watch over the wants
of the poor.

The Hospice-Général has been successively enlarged at different periods. Lately, they have made a considerable purchase of land, and erected vast buildings.
Its population is of about two thousand individuals. Although under the same administrative commission as the Hôtel-Dieu, it
has its particular director, who acts under

the superintendance of the commission,
which commission is subject to the public
administration.

The care of foundlings is one of the principal attributes of the Hospice-Général. Or-
phans, who are found without means
of existence, are brought up in the same
way as those who are abandoned; excepting, that they are maintained at the expence of the *communes* to which they be-
long; while at the same time the others are
chargeable to the departement; excepting
however the assistence of the communes.
The establishment provides the baby linen
and clothing for the use of the foundlings;
it likewise pays all the expenses of feeding
and education of these children, as long as
they remain in the hospital. When they are
sent into the country, the amount of board,
and nurses charges, till they attain the
age of twelve years, is paid out of the
funds of the departement. The Hospice —

General, receives each year on an average about five or six hundred foundlings. A *tour* is always ready at one of the entrances to receive them. Once a week, two coaches filled with these unfortunate little creatures, are sent off one into the country called the *pays de Bray*, the other to that called the *Roumois*, where they are left with agents who are charged to leave them with the nurses. In each of those *communes*, doctors are employed by the administrative commission to visit them in case of sickness.

We perceive, the front of the church of the hospital, from the boulevard Martainville. In 1785, the ancient chapel belonging to this hospital being found too small to contain the population, it became necessary to erect the present for that purpose. This church was dedicated on the 25th march 1790. The architecture has been much criticised. Perhaps more harmony on the whole might have been desirable; but nevertheless, the different parts of it are handsome, and the edifice, such as it is, still does honour to its author, the late Mr Vauquelin.

The principal entrance to this hospital is situated in the rue Bourgerue.

THE ASYLUM FOR THE INSANE,

Situated in the rue Saint-Julien, suburb of Saint-Sever.

The *frères de Saint-Yon*, having been invited, in 1705, to come and establish themselves in Rouen, by the archbishop Nicolas Colbert and the first president Nicolas Camus de Pont-Carré, they accordingly purchased the portion of ground, which bears their name, in 1708. They erected the church themselves without the assistance of an architect, even acting as masons and workmen. The first stone was laid on the 7th june 1728. This edifice is

12.

of remarkable execution. In the exterior, its elevation is about ninety six feet including a lantern of about thirty , which stands above the transept of the edifice. In the interior, the length is one hundred and twenty five feet and the breadth twenty five feet. On the 16th of july 1734, the *Frères de Saint-Yon,* carried with great pomp, to their church, the remains of their founder, the venerable Lasalle, who died in 1719, and was buried in the church of Saint-Sever. Independently of poor children, who were instructed by the monks according to their condition, they likewise received incorrigible children, who were sent by their parents to be taken care of; they also received a limited number of insane persons, thirty were habitually kept here at the expence of their families.

From the time when the *Frères de Saint-Yon ,* as also all other religious communities, were suppressed, untill 1820, the

house of Saint–Yon, became successivly a
revolutionary prison, a barrack, a *grenier
d'abondance*, or corn store house, a house
of detention for spanish prisoners, an hospital for wounded soldiers in 1814, and a
poor house. This last establishment was
one of the most considerable of this description ; but, it was suppressed in 1820, by
royal ordonance.

Already in the preceding year, the *Conseil général* of the departement of the Seine-
Inferieure had taken into consideration the
deplorable state, to which the unfortunate
insane were reduced, and they resolved to
alleviate their wretched condition. It had
been represented to them that these unfortunate people could not receive in the hospitals of Rouen, Havre or Dieppe, where there
where great numbers of them shut up, the
great attention, which their position required, or not even those which humanity demanded.

The *conseil général* on a proposition from
M. Malouet, then prefect of the departement, voted the establishment of a special
asylum for the insane belonging to the departement. The buildings and dependencies
of the ancient monastery of Saint-Yon were
designated as being fit for that purpose. The
situation of the place at the extremity of the
suburb, and in a healthy situation, and the
numerous plantations which it would be easy
to make in the large gardens which surround
the establishment, appeared as many fa-
vourable circumstances, to fix the choice of
the administration.

Therefore, in 1821, they entered into
a contract for the building of five different
courts for the treatement of insane persons.

On the 25th August 1822, on the feast of
Saint-Louis, the prefect M. de Vanssay laid
the first stone of the establishement.

From that time the works were carried on
with activity. Already in July 1825, fifty

seven patients had been admitted. This
asylum contains at this time, 390 boarders
and 150 poors at the charge of the departement.

It occupies a superficies of nine or ten
hectares. The inmates are taken care of by
the sisters of Saint-Joseph of Cluny.

The admirable order which reigns in the
establishment, the internal management to
which the insane are subjected, have already
attracted the attention of foreign medical
men, who are charged with the treatement
of the same malady in the hospitals of their
own countries. It may be said that this
asylum has, for several years served as a
model to all the others.

PRISONS.

There are two principal prisons in Rouen :
the *house of correction*, and the *maison de*

justice, in the court of the Palais—de—Justice. The first, commonly called *Bicêtre*, contains the debtors, prisoners accused but not tried, and those sentenced to imprisonment under twelve months; in the second those already convicted for crimes are confined. Those sentenced to more than twelve months are sent to the central depôt at Gaillon, ten leagues distant from Rouen.

According to a statement made by Mr Vingtrinier, the principal phisician of the prisons, the average of the population of the house of correction is about three hundred; that of the *maison de justice* about ninety; the mortality about one in fifty nine, in the first, and one in sixty eight, in the second.

●●●

SOLDIERS BARRACKS.

There are three different barracks in Rouen : the first is situated near the *quai aux Meules* at Saint-Sever, and contains about one thousand men. The second on the Champ-de-Mars, and contains about seven hundred and fifty men. The third is the *caserne Bonne-Nouvelle*; situated in the suburb of Saint-Sever. Most people pass the ancient priory of *Bonne-Nouvelle* (so named by Queen Matilda, on receiving the news of the victory of Hastings), and see only a barrack. To the monks who formely inhabited this ancient priory, cuirassiers, dragoons and foot soldiers have succeeded.

The barracks of *Bonne-Nouvelle* will contain about three hundred cavalry or about six hundred infantry.

ᎧᎧᎧᎧᎧᎧᎧᎧᎧᎧᎧᎧᎧᎧᎧᎧᎧᎧᎧᎧᎧᎧᎧᎧᎧᎧᎧᎧ

REMARKABLE EDIFICES.

—

HÔTEL DU BOURGTHEROULDE,
Place de la Pucelle.

After the cathedral and Saint-Ouen, this town possesses no other monument which excites more the curiosity of french or English antiquarians. The first person who described the famous bas—reliefs of the *Camp du Drap—d'Or*, which ornament the exterior of the ancient gallery of the edifice, is dom Montfaucon in the 4th volume of his *Monuments of the french Monarchy.* He only did it, on the indications given by the abbé Noel, who gave the first explanations of these sculptures. After Montfaucon came Dr Ducarel, who has only copied the learned benedictine. Dibdin, the British an-

tiquarian, has also paid his tribute of admiration to the hotel du Bourgtheroulde, in his
*Bibliographical, antiquarian and pictures-
que tour through France.* Cotman and Daw-
son Turner, his countrymen, have given a
place to this edifice in their respective pu-
blications. M. de Jolimont, in his *most
remarquable monuments in the town of
Rouen* devotes an article and two engravings
to this edifice. MM. Nodier, Taylor and
de Cailleux have enriched ther *picturesque
and romantic tour*, with a collection of li-
thographic engravings representing the celebrated interview between Francis I[st] and
Henry VIIIth, that took place in 1520 in
a field situated between Guines and Ardres
in Picardy. M[r] A. Le Prevost has also written
learned memoirs on the hotel du Bourgtheroulde. He has fixed the date of the building
(about the end of the XV century), and
revealed the name of the founder (Guillaume-
le-Roux), and facilitated the numerous des-

13

criptions which have been made of it. The
most complete, is that given by M. Dela-
quérière, in his work entitled : *Historical
description of the houses of Rouen.*

In the short description that we give of
this remarkable building, we must notice
the bas-reliefs, six in number, which adorn
the elegant hexagonal tower, in the inner
court and represent pastoral scenes. We must
also add that interpreters make a great mis-
take when they inform strangers that the
celebrated maid of Orleans (burnt in 1431)
was judged and imprisoned in this building.

ANCIENT ABBEY OF SAINT AMAND,
Rue Saint-Amand.

NON EST HIC ALIVD NISI DOMVS DEI.

The pious monks who caused this simple
and touching inscription to be engraven over
the gate of their monastery, never supposed
that one day it would offer the most strange

of *solecisms*. Enter this house and you will
have great difficulty in believing that you
visit one of the most celebrated abbeys in
Rouen.

This abbey, which was founded and endo-
wed by the pious lady Aimeline, and enriched by the liberalities of Robert-the-Ma-
gnificent, this once famous monastery,
which was honoured by the protection of
kings, is now a confused sort of inclosure
and inhabited by workmen of different
kinds. Dirty courts and buildings in ruin
have been for a long time the only remains
of the interior of Saint-Amand. Some parts
nevertheless have escaped destruction. Such
is a very curious building, which had been
erected about the end of the XVIth century
during the life of the abbot Thomasse Daniel.
This edifice is extremely remarkable from
the sculptures which cover the whole front,
and chiefly represent pointed windows. On
the first floor, we find a room with two fire

places, on one we may still distinguish in
spite of mutilation, the armorial bearings of
the Daniel family. The wainscot is even
more curious than the sculptures which ornament the front of the house. At one of the
corners of this building there is a small
turret, of stone, its form is polygonal; its
ornaments are rich and in very good taste:
it is a fine specimen of the productions of the
renaissance.

The building, with a front of the Ionic order, which is separated from the
other by the turret of which we have just
spoken, contains a room, which a few
years ago, excited the curiosity of connoisseurs. The fire place was surmounted by an
oaken wainscot, which represented, in
niches separated by pilasters, four figures,
those of the virgin, the angel Gabriel, Saint-
Margaret and Saint-Magdalen.

BUREAU DES FINANCES,

Opposite the front of the Cathedral.

This was the ancient *Palace of the Court des Aides.* The building is principally composed of hewn stone : it was built about the year 1509. Although this edifice has suffered numerous degradations, it still merits the attention of connais-seurs. The building has two separate fronts : the principal one opposite the cathedral, the other in the *rue du Petit-Salut.* The decorations are the same on both.

In 1705, the *Cour des Aides* was united to the *Cour des Comptes,* under the name *Cour des Comptes, Aides et Finances de Rouen.* The present edifice has nevertheless always retained the name of *Bureau des Finances.*

13

REMARKABLE HOUSES AND CELE-
BRATED MEN.

Ancient town hall, rue de la Grosse-
Horloge and rue Thouret.

Sculptured wooden houses, Grande-Rue,
n° 115 and 129.

House, rue aux Juifs, n° 47 and 49.

House, rue Percière, n° 11.

House, rue Bouvreuil, n° 4.

House, rue Étoupée, n° 4.

Houses, rue des Carmes, n° 69 to 77.

House, rue Caquerel, n° 13.

House, rue Damiette, n° 29.

Houses, rue Eau-de-Robec, n°° 186,
221, 223.

Houses, rue Malpalu. n° 90 and 92.

Houses, rue du Change, n° 2 to 8.

Houses, rue du Bac, n° 28 and 30.

House, rue des Cordeliers, n° 45.

Houses which are remarkable as having

been those in which the following celebrated
men were born.

House in the rue de la Pie, n° 4, where
in 1606 the great Corneille was born.

House in the rue des Bons – Enfants,
n° 132-134, where Fontenelle, was born
on the 11th february 1657.

House in the rue aux Ours, n° 61. An
inscription placed on this house reminds us,
that it was here, that A. Boieldieu, the celebrated composer, was born.

House rue aux Juifs, n° 9. Here Jean
Jouvenet, the celebrated painter, was born
on the 21st August, 1647.

To these celebrated names we must add
the following of men equally natives of
Rouen : Thomas Corneille (the brother of
Peter), Lémery, Basnage, Samuel Bochart,
the fathers Berruyer, Brumoy, Daniel,
Sanadon, the painters Restout, Letellier,
Sacquepée, Colombel, Lemonnier, Geri-
cault, mademoiselle Champmeslé, madame

Du Boccage, Armand Carrel, Edward Adam, Dulong. Rouen is the birth-place of many other distinguished men.

•••

BRIDGES.

—

STONE BRIDGE AND STATUE
OF CORNEILLE.

This bridge was opened to the public, in 1829. It is about one hundred and fifty yards higher up than the bridge of boats, which was formerly almost opposite the *rue du Bac* [1]. We may almost say that it is formed of two separate bridges, of which the two ends join each other on the western

---

[1] Erected in 1626, it was demolished in september 1836.

extremity of the *Ile Lacroix*. Each part of
the bridge is composed of three arches.
The span of the middle arch is of thirty
one mètres (93 feet french) ; the lateral arches, are of twenty six mètres (78 feet); the
whole length of the bridge is two hundred
and sixty six mètres (798 feet). In the centre
of the platform on the bridge, is placed the
bronze statue of Pierre Corneille, on a
pedestal of white Carrara marble, which
rests on a base of granite.

This statue is twelve feet high, and weighs
4540 kilogrammes (9274 pounds *de marc*).
It was cast by Mr Honoré Gonon, at Paris,
after the model by Mr David. The pedestal
is by Mr Grégoire, the civil architect of
the Seine–Inférieure. The height of the
monument is twenty six feet. The first stone
was laid by the king, on the 10th september
1833. The statue was solemnly inaugurated,
on the 19 october 1834. On one side of the
pedestal, we distinguish the following inscription :

TO PIERRE CORNEILLE,
BY SUBSCRIPTION,
1834.

This statue was erected by means of a subscription, opened by the Society of Emulation of Rouen. It is to this society that we owe the first idea of this national monument.

A medal was struck for the occasion, and represents on one side the head of *Pierre Corneille*, with the following inscription:

Pierre Corneille, born at Rouen the 6th june 1606, died at Paris on the 1st october 1684.

And on the reverse, the statue, with this inscription:

Statue of bronze, erected by subscription to Pierre Corneille in his native town, through the exertions of the Society of Emulation of Rouen, in 1834.

SUSPENSION BRIDGE.

The numerous commercial trading vessels, which come up the Seine, were formerly obliged to wait several days, before they could get along side the quay to discharge. It became essential to enlarge the port, for which reason the stone bridge, at the entrance to the town, was built; but this arrangment rendered another bridge indispensable; and in 1828, the town council consulted on the possibility of removing the bridge of boats farther down; but the bad state it was in, and the enormous sum it cost to keep it in repair, and the length of time it took to open it for the passage of vessels, at once caused them to give up all idea of this old machine, formerly looked upon as a wonder; but, which did not now answer the purpose.

On the 8th of june 1834, a royal ordinance was issued, approving the under-

taking. At last MM. Seguin brothers, civil
engineers, and Pierre Colin, undertaker of
public works, were, on the 16th october
1834, declared the approved contractors
for the erection of the bridge; at the same
time granting to them the receipts of the tolls
for a period of 99 years, the bridge to be
terminated at the latest, by the 1st of january
1837. And it was entirely completed by the
1st september 1836 (the very day the bridge
of boats was suppressed). At the expiration
of the 99 years, the bridge will become the
property of the government. Its breadth is
seven metres thirty centimetres, its length
197 metres, and the whole expense has
amounted to 750,000 fr. On the left of the
bridge is situated a guard house, and on
the right Brune's house, erected by the
city as a reward for courage and devotedness
on many occasions.

●●

RIVER AND RIVULETS.

—

THE RIVER SEINE.

The source of the Seine is to be found near the hamlet of Envergeraux, and about two leagues and half from the village of Saint-Seine, in Burgundy. After a course of more than 200 leagues from east to west, it falls into the Ocean, between Havre and Honfleur [1].

The depth of the Seine at Rouen allows this town to be classed amongst the principal ports of France. They calculate at from

---

[1] See : *Voyage from Havre to Rouen;* and *Excursion from Rouen to Paris*, *by the Seine.* Rouen, 1839, in-18vo, with maps and plates.

14

2000 to 2500 the number of vessels of all sizes, which annually come this port.

ROBEC.

This rivulet has its source near the village of *Fontaine-sous-Préaux*, about two leagues from Rouen, runs through five *communes*, and enters Rouen by the suburb Saint-Hilaire; passing through the town, it falls into the Seine, near the stone bridge.

AUBETTE.

The Aubette has its source at Saint-Aubin, a small village near Rouen. This rivulet runs through *Saint-Léger-du-bourg-Denis, Darnétal*, enters Rouen by the suburb Martainville, and falls into the Seine, at the entrance to the *Cours-Dauphin,* near the porte *Guillaume-Lion.* These two rivers are specially useful for mills and dying establishments.

RENELLE.

If the etymology of the name *Renelle* is doubtful, the utility of the stream at least is not so. It supplies numerous tanneries, of which there are still a great many in the street which bears its name. This sort of industry is very ancient in Rouen, and has never been established in any other part of the town. On the 22nd of march 1560, the parliament issued an act, ordering all the tanners to remove their establishments to the *Eau-de-Robec* ; but, they said that they required clear water to carry on their trade, and therefore, were allowed, by order of the king, to remain on the Renelle. This rivulet comes from the Gaalor spring, and flows from the fountain of the *Bailliage*, almost in a straight line to the Seine, into which it falls.

●●●

FOUNTAINS.

—

The more churches there were in a town, there should be as many public fountains. Under the ancient law, a tub was placed at the entrance of the temples, in which the priests washed their hands and feet; under the new, and in imitation, fountains were placed near the churches, where the christians; before entering, washed their face and hands. This remark was applicable especially, in Rouen, before the revolution, where the number of churches and fountains was quite equal. There are not now thirty seven parochial churches; but we can still count thirty six public fountains, not including those in many private houses.

Of all these fountains, only seven merit

particular attention, from their architectural
and historical character. They are the fountains of the *Croix-de-Pierre*, the *Crosse*,
the *Grosse-Horloge*, the *Vieux-Marché*,
the *Pucelle*, *Saint-Maclou*, and *Lisieux*.

FOUNTAIN OF THE CROIX-DE-PIERRE,

Carrefour Saint-Vivien.

There formerly existed, not far from the
fountain known at present under the name
of the *Croix-de-Pierre* (stone cross), a cross,
which had been raised through the piety of
the inhabitants; but, we now can find no
authentic document of the period of its
being erected; all we know is that it had
been rebuilt in the year 1628.

This fountain is composed of three partitions in the form of a pyramid, and is ornamented with some statues; its appearance is
exceedingly fine. One may still form an idea
of the beauty of its architecture, in spite of

14.

its ruinous condition, and even the repairs
it has undergone.

FOUNTAIN OF THE CROSSE,

*At the corner of the streets des Carmes, and
de l'Hopital.*

This is a small monument in the gothic style
of the end of the XV.th century. The sculptures which decorate it, are remarkable for
their fineness and delicacy. It is surmounted
by a royal crown. Its name comes from its
being situated at the corner of the house,
which had for sign the crozier belonging to
the monks of *Notre-Dame de l'Ile-Dieu.*

Some etymologists see in the word *Crosse,*
an alteration of the english word *cross.* In
the year 1815, this fountain was completely renewed.

FOUNTAIN OF THE GROSSE-HORLOGE,

*At the corner of the streets des Vergetiers,
and the Grande-Rue.*

FOUNTAIN OF THE VIEUX-MARCHÉ,
On the old market place.

A modern square building, of the doric order. It was erected by Mr Bouet, an architect of Rouen.

FOUNTAINS OF SAINT-MACLOU, AND
OF THE PUCELLE.

Strangers will be repaid for their trouble in going to see these fountains. The first, is situated at the corner of the church of Saint-Maclou; there remain still two figures of children, an elegant creation of Jean Goujon. We mention the second, the *fountain of the Pucelle,* on the place of the same name, on account of the historical recollections, which are attached to it. It is a heavy composition of Paul Slodtz. Its want of style causes us to regret the beautiful triangular fountain, which was erected after the execution, in this square, of the *heroine of Vaucouleurs*, a monument which instead of destroying, they should have tried to preserve.

FOUNTAIN OF LISIEUX,
Rue de la Savonnerie.

This fountain is by far the most remarkable of the whole. It is thus named on account of its being erected against a house, which belonged to the bishop of Lisieux, who lodged in it when he came to Rouen. At the top of the pyramid, we may remark Apollo, dressed in a most extraordinary manner, and represented playing on the harp. Under the god of the poets, we distinguish the horse Pegasus. Immediatly beneath, a figure with three heads is represented, of which the manuscripts make a *philosophy* [1]. *The nine muses are distributed*

---

[1] According to these manuscripts, the three heads represent *Logic*, *Philosophy* and *Metaphysics*. They were surmonted by a crown.

in the rest of the masonry, under the figure
with three heads, which might almost be that
of a Hecate. Rocks, trees, turf and sheep,
form the accompaniements of this *Mount-*
Parnassus.

The water ran formerly from two brass
figures of Salamanders, which indicated the
date of the time of Francis the first. Mutilated as it is, this monument is still very
curious, and merits to be visited. Its erection dates from the year 1518.

●●

MINERAL WATERS.

Rouen has also its mineral waters, which,
even in the neighbouring towns, have a sort
of reputation. I will point out three of the
principal sources, after *Lepecq de la Clô-*
ture : The first, to the east, is known under
the name of *la Marèquerie*, to which we
arrive by the rue Martainville; the second,

to the south east, named *de Saint-Paul*; the third is situated at *Déville*, in the neighbourhood of Rouen. The learned doctor, on whose authority I speak, assures us that sick people to whom he ordered the water of the last named spring, were cured by the use of it. He also adds, that this spring might become very valuable to the inhabitants of the western quarter of the town. Nevertheless, it has never been much known, and even at the present day very few people are acquainted with its existence.

●●

SQUARES AND MARKET PLACES.

OLD MARKET AND PLACE DE LA PUCELLE.

The name of the first of these two places points out to us that it is the most ancient in

Rouen; it is also the most considerable. It existed in the XIth century, and was at that period, situated in the suburb. Formerly, it covered a much larger space of ground than at present; since, in the XVIth century, it occupied the whole of the ground contained between the *rue du Vieux-Palais,* the church of Saint-Eloi and Saint-Michael; the last mentioned church has disappeared within the last few years, and is replaced by a handsome building, which is named the *Hôtel Saint-Michel.* About the commencement of the XVIth century, the houses in the neighbourhood of the church of Saint-Eloi and the *rue du Vieux-Palais,* were erected; one of them still remains, it is the Hôtel du Bourgtheroulde, which I have already described. The old market was thus divided into two unequal parts. The spot where the innocent *Joan of Arc* was burnt in 1431, retains the name of *place de la Pucelle.* It is also called *place du Marché-aux-Veaux,* on account of its

former destination. It is then on the old
market place, that the French heroine was
sacrificed to the superstition of that age.

NEW MARKET.

Fruit, eggs, cream cheeses, or small
Neufchâtel cheeses : such are the supplies
to be found in this market. About fifty years
ago, a gilt leaden statue, representing Louis
XVth in his youth, and covered with the
royal mantle, was to be seen. This monument has been replaced by the present obelisk, which furnishes an abundant supply
of water to the inhabitants of this quarter.

PLACE NOTRE-DAME.

Before 1429, this place served as a poultry and grass market. In 1537, it was paved
and enclosed with a low wall. In 1641, two
stone Crosses, still visible in some ancient
engravings, were placed at the two corners.

In the time of *Pommeraye*, the *parvis* Notre-
Dame, was the place on which bonfires were
lighted. At present it is the flower and seed
market, regularly held on the sundays and
fridays.

PLACE DE LA CALENDE.

It was formerly called *Port-Morant*, *port
des navires*, or *port de Notre-Dame*, because, before the first dukes enclosed the
Seine within certain limits, the vessels dis-
charged their cargoes at this place. The house
which is exactly opposite the porch of the
church and on which we distinguish a dial,
is the remains of the old *Hôtel-Dieu*.

THE ROUGEMARE.

In the year 949, Otho, emperor of Germany, Louis IV.th, king of France, and Ar-
nold, count of Flanders, laid siege to the
town of Rouen. The duke Richard I.st, surnamed *Sans-Peur*, made a *sortie* by the

15

porte Beauvoisine, and fell on the enemies of which he made a great slaughter. This action took place partly on the site of the present *Rouge-Mare* (red-pool), from the blood with which it was covered.

In 1450, the *Rouge-Mare* became the horse market, which has, since the end of the last century, been transferred to the *Boulingrin*. The *Rouge-Mare* is now the butter market.

THE BOULINGRIN.

The English have returned to the French that which they had borrowed of them. Formerly, people did not go to walk on the *boulevard*, but on the *boule-verd*, from which the english have made *bowling-green*, a literal translation. From this word, the french derive their *Boulingrin*.

This place is situated at the junction of the rampes Beauvoisine and Saint-Hilaire; it is a vast square surrounded by a maguificcnt double row of horse chesnut trees. Since the horse market has been transferred to it, people commonly call it the *new Rouge-Mare*.

●●

PUBLIC LIBRARY,

PICTURE GALLERY AND MUSEUMS.

———

PUBLIC LIBRARY,

At the Town Hall.

The opening of this library took place on the 4th july 1809. Since then, the inhabitants and strangers are admitted into this establishment every day, (except sundays, thursdays and during the vacations), from eleven till four, and from 6 till 9 o'clock in the evening. The present collection, consists

of about thirty five thousand volumes. There
are above eleven hundred manuscripts.
Several of them are very curious and rare,
from their date, their illuminations, or their
subjects. Amongst the first, although not
the most ancient, I will mention the famous
Gradual by Daniel d'Aubonne, who died
in the year 1714. It measures two feet seven
inches in length by one foot ten inches in
breadth and weighs seventy three pounds.
It is ornamented with brass plates; on
each side of the binding, we may observe
the armorial bearings of the abbey of Saint-
Ouen, which are also of brass. This manuscript contains about two hundred vignettes,
initials of all sizes, and also a great number
of gilt letters. One cannot admire too much
the patience of the author, who passed thirty
years, it is said, on this immense underta-
king. The library contains also other manuscripts, infinitely more precious, amongst
which are several of the XIth, IXth, and even

of the VIIth and VIIIth centuries. The learned will distinguish amongst the most important of the manuscripts, the curious missal of archbishop Robert, which was brought from England about the year 1050, with the *benedictionary*, which was used at the coronation of the Anglo-Saxon Kings. These two manuscripts are ornamented with magnificent miniatures in the greek style of the empire. The books printed before the year 1500 amount to three hundred and twenty eight, of which two hundred and forty bear dates; the most ancient is of 1468.

The library contains also collections of great value and editions which have become very rare. The government has enriched it with several very valuable works. The most important gift that has yet been made to the library, is that which was sent, by the commission of records in England, of the collection of historical documents, which

15.

they have published. This magnificent gift,
which will be followed by several others, is
composed of 71 vols. folio, and 168 vols. 8vo.

The Leber's magnificent collection of books
and manuscripts, bought last year by the city,
will shortly be added to the public library.

The present keeper is M. A. Pottier.

PICTURE GALLERY,

At the Town Hall.

The opening of the picture gallery took
place on the same day (4th july 1809), as
that of the library. The greater part of the
paintings have been collected in the departement. The government has also assisted in
enriching it, by giving several paintings of
different schools, the municipal council by
voting different acquisitions, and some
private persons, by voluntary gifts. This
interesting collection is composed of about
three hundred paintings, amongst which

we remark *a Virgin in the midst of Angels*, called *the Virgin of Saint-Sixte*, by Raphael, an admirable copy, if not a second original of the picture known under the same name in the gallery of Dresden; also three small paintings, placed next to each other, and which are incontestably by that great painter and in his best style; the Van Eyck representing *the Virgin in the midst of young girls; a mass during the league*, a painting which is curious on account of the subject and great personnages which it represents; *a Conversion of saint Matthew*, by Valentin; *a saint Francis in prayer*, by Hannibal Carrache; *an Ecce Homo* and a copy of the *Holy family*, by Mignard; *a death of saint Francis*, by Jouvenet; several marines, by Vernet; *a descent from the Cross*, by Lahire; *the plague of Milan*, by Lemonnier, of Rouen; and a great many others, which it would require too much room to mention here. At the ex-

tremity of the entrance gallery, we remark a
statue of baked clay by Caffiery [1], representing Pierre Corneille. Several marble
statues and plaster castes of the finest ancient
statues, are placed in the room at the extremity of this gallery. The statues which we
observe in the lobby are those of general
Bonchamps, by David, and opposite, that
of Achilles, by Bougron. The latter belongs
to the academy, which possesses also the magnificent painting by Mr Court, representing
Corneille complimented in the theatre by the
great Condé and the fine *portrait of Boiel-*
dieu, by Mr Boullenger de Boisfremont.
These two paintings are placed in the hall
of the academy, adjoining that of the library
and picture gallery; strangers are permitted
to see them.

----

[1] Another statue of Corneille, in marble, is
placed in the large hall on the ground floor; it is a
much esteemed work of Cortot, a french sculptor.

During the month of July, there is an exhibition of paintings, principally by artists of Rouen.

The establishment is open to the public on sundays and thursdays, and every day to painters and strangers, from ten till four o'clock.

The present keeper is M. H. Bellangé.

MUSEUM OF ANTIQUITIES.

At Saint-Mary's, rue Poussin.

This museum, which was established in 1833, after a proposition of M⁺ Dupont-Delporte, prefect, by the general council of the departement, was opened to the public in 1834. It occupies two of the galleries of the cloister of the ancient convent of Saint-Mary. In the first gallery are the gallic, roman and gallo-roman antiquities, as also those of the middle ages; in the second, those of the period, termed the *renaissance*

This chronological order has been preserved as much as possible. The searches wich have taken place in different parts of the departement, and especially in the roman theatre at Lillebonne, have produced the greater number of antiquities. A great many others are through the generosity of private individuals. This museum contains statues, busts, bas-reliefs, fragments of architecture, sarcophagi, urns of marble and stone; vases of bronze, glass and baked earth; gallic and roman medals, pieces of french coins, seals of the middle ages, stained glass, arms, pieces of furniture, utensils and ornaments of different ages.

This museum is open on sundays and holy days from eleven till four o'clock, and on tuesdays and thursdays for amateurs and strangers, from twelve till three o'clock.

The keeper is Mr A. Deville.

MUSEUM OF NATURAL HISTORY.

At Saint-Mary's, rue Poussin.

The municipal administration of Rouen founded the gallery of natural history, in 1827; but, it was only in the year 1832, and after having been enriched by the administration of that time, that it was judged fit to be offered to public curiosity.

The increase of this museum has been rapid; already, within its few years of existence, it may be advantageously compared with most provincial collections; and through the maritime situation of the town, may one day be placed immediately after that at Paris. It is remarkable, for the numerous shells which it possesses, as also for some mammiferi, which are exceedingly rare. This gallery is open to the public, on sundays and holy days; foreigners and students may enter on any day.

Mr Pouchet is the director of this establishment.

●●

LEARNED SOCIETIES.

————

ROYAL ACADEMY OF SCIENCES, ARTS AND BELLES-
LETTRES.

——

FREE SOCIETY OF EMULATION.

——

CENTRAL SOCIETY OF AGRICULTURE.

——

SOCIETY FOR THE IMPROVEMENT OF COMMERCE
AND INDUSTRY.

——

SOCIETY OF MEDICINE.

——

APOTHECARIES SOCIETY.

SOCIETY OF THE FRIENDS OF ARTS.

HORTICULTURAL SOCIETY.

COMMISSION OF ANTIQUITIES.

PHILHARMONIC SOCIETY.

BOTANICAL GARDEN.

This garden was formerly situated on the *Cours-Dauphin;* but, the municipal administration wishing to render that portion of the town named Martainville, more healthy, entertained the project of opening a street at the entrance of the town, on the ground occupied by this garden ; in consequence they sought another place, more suitable for a botanical garden. The place fixed upon, is the *park of Trianon*, where people formerly went, to visit the fine hot houses, and rare

16

collection of dahlias and other plants, which belonged to a distinguished english florist, Mr Calvert.

This new botanical garden, is situated at the extremity of the rue d'Elbeuf, and forms a square of about 45,500 metres (or yards) surface. Mr Lejeune, an architect, gave the plan of this garden.

LECTURES ON CHEMISTRY.

These lectures take place every year, (beginning the 15th november), on tuesdays and saturdays at one o'clock, in one of the halls of the ancient convent of Saint-Marie. The lectures are principally on the application of chemistry to arts and industry.

LECTURES ON NATURAL PHILOSOPHY.

These lectures were instituted in 1835; they take place twice a week in the amphitheatre at Saint-Marie.

PUBLIC LESSONS IN DRAWING.

This school, founded by Mr Descamps, the author of the *lives of flemish painters*, is now established at Saint-Marie. The lessons commence in the month of november and finish in the month of august, from one o'clock till three.

LECTURES ON NATURAL HISTORY.

They take place in the amphitheatre, which is given for this science, and is situated at Saint-Marie, Poussin street. The lectures take place on tuesdays and saturdays, during the winter, at eight o'clock in the evening.

There are besides, at Saint-Marie, every sunday, lectures on geometry and mechanics applied to arts and manufactures, and lectures also on commercial law and book keeping.

SECONDARY SCHOOL OF MEDICINE.

The different branches are taught in the hospitals, by the physicians who are attached to these establishments.

●●●

THEATRES.

—

The *Théâtre-des-Arts* at the corner of the rues *Grand-Pont* and des *Charrettes,* was erected by Francis Gueroult, an architect of Rouen. The first stone was laid on the 18th june 1774, and the opening took place the 29th june 1776, on Saint-Peter's day and the fête of Corneille. This theatre was altered and lighted with gas, in 1835, and will contain about seventeen or eighteen hundred persons. The ceiling was painted

by Lemoine, a native of this city, and represents the *apotheosis of Corneille*.

The peristyle fronting the rue des Charrettes is in the form of a quarter of a circle
and is composed of columns of the ionic
order. The medallion of Pierre Corneille is
sculptured on the entablature which is supported by these columns, and on each side
of the medallion, we perceive Melpomene
with a dagger, and Thalia with a mask.

The performers for operas and comedies
are generally good.

The second theatre is situated on the old
market place and is called the *Théâtre-
Français;* this building formerly used as
a tennis court, was opened for theatrical
purposes on the 2nd of february 1793. This
theatre will contain about twelve hundred
persons. Besides these two theatres, there
is a third at the entrance of Saint-Sever,
which is the circus or *Ambigu-Dramatique*.

16.

●●●

PUBLIC WALKS IN ROUEN.

———

COURS BOIELDIEU AND THE EXCHANGE.

These are the fashionable walks. The
bronze statue between the two is that of
Boieldieu, the celebrated french composer
a native of Rouen. It is the work of the
sculptor Dantan the younger.

COURS DE LA REINE.

According to *Farin*, this public walk was
formed for a walk for the ladies, and is one
of the finest in the kingdom; its length
is about 674 fathoms. Four rows of large
elms form the whole length on the banks

of the Seine. On holy-thursday, the *Cours-de-la-Reine* begins to be used as a fashionable promenade, and it may be said that on that day, it has a very gay appearance.

AVENUES OF MONT-RIBOUDET, AND COURS-DAUPHIN.

The first is the principal entrance to Rouen from Havre and Dieppe, and the second, at the opposite extremity of the quay, the entrance from Paris, Evreux, etc.

THE BOULEVARDS.

They occupy, for the greater part, the place of the ditches which surrounded the town; they were planted between the years 1770 and 1780 and were paved in 1783, at the expense of the town. They are about 3 miles in length.

WALKS WITHOUT THE TOWN.

Mount Saint–Catherine first presents itself. We may go to it, either by the Paris high road, or by the *petites eaux* Martainville. The last mentioned, although the least frequented, is perhaps the preferable route on account of the diversity of the landscape.

It will be useless for the traveller, when he has reached the top of the hill, to look for the ancient abbey of the *Sainte-Trinité–du-Mont*, the chapel of the *priory of Saint-Michel*, or the fortifications, in which the marquis of Villars withstood the attacks of Henry IVth; nothing of them remains at the present day, except two remnants of a wall, which threaten to fall on the traveller, who is imprudent enough to approach too near them.

From this elevated position, in turning towards the north-east, we see the valley of *Darnetal*, which has become so rich

through the industry of those who inhabit it.
The eye reposes with pleasure on the gothic tower of the church of *Carville;* and
of which, according to tradition, Henry IVth,
made a post of observation when he besieged
the fort of the *ligue.* We must not forget
that an English detachment, which served
in the army of the king, conducted itself
very bravely in the different attacks, with
which it was entrusted. On the opposite side
of the valley of Darnetal and towards the
north, we distinguish the hill named *des Sa-
pins,* on which the monumental burying
ground is situated. This latter hill adjoins
the *Bois-Guillaume* from which also the
view is admirable although inferior to
that from the mount Saint-Catherine, which
advances like a promontory, above the
immense valley of the Seine, while that
of Bois-Guillaume or Beauvoisine, recedes
from the circular line formed by the union
of these different hills.

The Bois-Guillaume joins *Saint-Aignan*.
We cross the latter *commune*, on our way to
Mont-aux-Malades, formerly the *Mont-
Saint-Jacques*. Antiquarians will not fail
to go and see a church at this place, which
is a venerable remains of norman architecture. There were two, but the other is
now almost destroyed. Travellers should
also visit the hill of *Canteleu* from which
the view is very fine, and at the same time
the country house of M. Élie Lefebure, called
the *Chateau of Canteleu*.

●●

BURYING GROUNDS OF ROUEN.

There are at present, five burying grounds
for the roman catholics, and two for the
protestants. They are the burying grounds
of *Saint-Gervais*, *Beauvoisine*, *Val-de-*

la-Jatte, of which a part has been walled
off for the protestants; *Mont-Gargan, Saint-
Sever*, and *Champ-des-Oiseaux*, which
latter forms the second protestant burying
ground. The great demand of families, to
obtain a piece of ground, on which to erect
a monument on the tomb of a relation, had
caused a great diminution of ground for in-
terments; the municipal administration therefore took measures to prevent the conse-
quences of it. On the proposition of the
marquis de Martainville, then mayor of the
town they determined, on the 24th april 1823,
that a monumental burying should be established on the east of Rouen, on a portion of
the hill of Fir-Trees which was barren,
and could be disposed of without any loss.

This new burying ground contains about
ten acres of ground, enclosed with walls. A
chapel is erected on the highest point of the
hill; and a vault has been formed under it
for the provisional deposit of bodies, which

cannot be interred immediately. A tariff
exists, which regulates the sum to be paid
by families, who wish to purchase a place
in this burying ground.

THE END.

ROUEN
1829

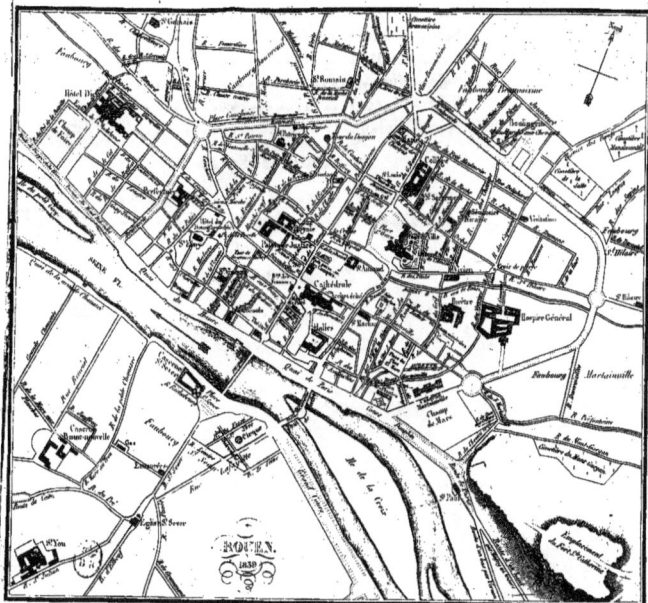

À ROUEN chez FRÈRE, Libraire. Sur le Port, N.º 45.

Benoist J.ᵉʳ à Paris.

CONTENTS.

17

CIVIL MONUMENTS.

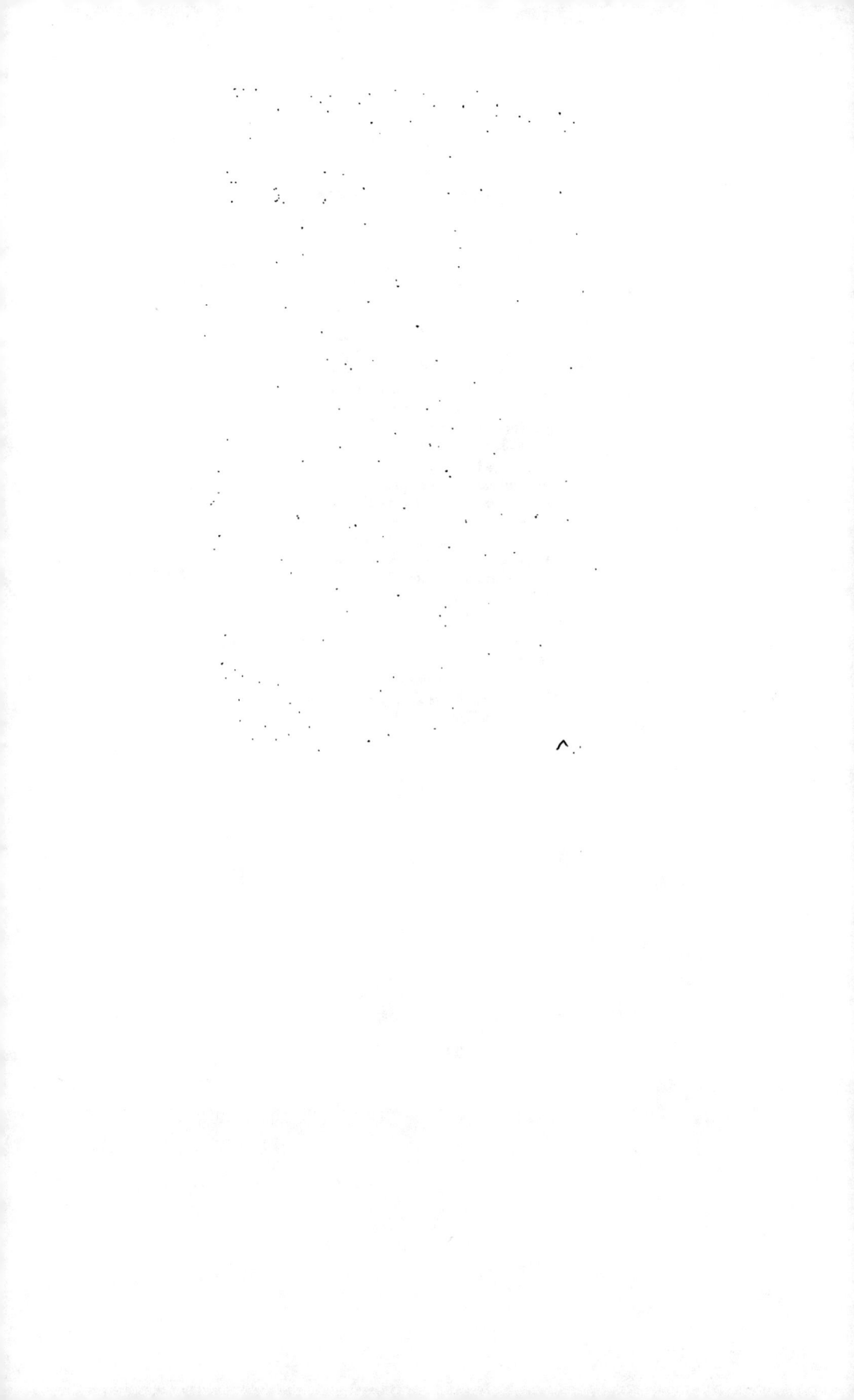

EDWARD FRERE,

PUBLISHER AND BOOKSELLER,

45, QUAI DE PARIS, ROUEN.

BOOKS

RELATING TO THE HISTORY OF ROUEN AND NORMANDY.

Histoire de Normandie, depuis les temps les plus reculés jusqu'à la conquête de l'Angleterre en 1066; par Th. Licquet; — précédée d'une Introduction sur la littérature, la mythologie, les mœurs des hommes du Nord; par G.-B. Depping. — 1835, 2 vol. in-8, avec une carte...   13 fr.

Histoire de la Normandie sous le règne de Guillaume-le-Conquérant et de ses successeurs, depuis la conquête de l'Angleterre jusqu'à la réunion de la Normandie au royaume de France; par G.-B. Depping, auteur de l'*Histoire des expéditions maritimes des Normands.* — 1835, 2 vol. in-8..................   13 fr.

Résumé de l'Histoire de Normandie, par Dubois. — 1825. In-18.............   2

Géologie de la Seine-Inférieure, par A. Passy. — 1832. In-4, et atlas........   20

Histoire de la ville de Dieppe et de ses environs; par Vitet. — 1833. 2 vol. in-8.   12

17.

(198)

Essai historique sur Louviers, par P. Dibon. — 1836. In-8 , fig.............   5

Essai historique et statistique sur la ville de Bolbec, par Collen-Castaigne. — In-8 , fig..............................   4 50

Itinéraire de Paris au Havre ; par Vaysse de Villiers. — in-8 , avec trois cartes..   3

Notice historique sur l'Académie des Palinods , par Ballin. — 1834. In-8 , fig..   3

Le Roman de Rou et des ducs de Normandie , par Robert Wace , publié , pour la première fois , d'après les manuscrits de France et d'Angleterre , avec des notes pour servir à l'intelligence du texte , par F. Pluquet. — 1827. 2 vol. in-8 , fig...   10

Observations philologiques et grammaticales sur le Roman de Rou et sur quelques règles de la langue des Trouvères au XIIᵉ siècle , par Raynouard. — *Dans le même volume* : Supplément aux notes historiques sur le Roman de Rou, par Aug. Le Prevost. — 1829. In-8 ......   3 50

Notice sur la vie et les écrits de Robert Wace , par F. Pluquet. — 1824. Grand in-8 , fig.........................   3

Contes populaires, préjugés, patois, proverbes , noms de lieux de l'arrondissement de Bayeux, publiés par F. Pluquet. — 1834. In-8 , fig.................   3 50

mière fois d'après les manuscrits de Londres, de Cambridge, de Bruxelles, de Douai et de Paris; par Francisque Michel. 1836-40. 3 vol. in-8............ 18

Les Chroniques de Normandie, publiées d'après un manuscrit du XIIIᵉ siècle de la Bibliothèque du Roi; par Francisque Michel. — 1839. In-4, avec miniature, cart............................. 15

Works on different subjects.

Le Roman de Brut, par Robert Wace, poète normand du XIIᵉ siècle, publié pour la première fois d'après les manuscrits des bibliothèques de Paris, avec un commentaire et des notes, par Leroux de Lincy. — 1836-38. 2 vol. in-8, fig..... 20 fr.

Histoire des Anglo-Saxons, de sir Francis Palgrave; traduit de l'anglais par Alexandre Licquet. — 1836. In-8, fig.. 7 50

Fragments littéraires de lady Jane Grey, reine d'Angleterre, avec la traduction, précédés d'une notice sur la vie et les écrits de cette femme célèbre; par Ed. Frère. — 1832. In-8, portrait........ 4

Cours de littérature à l'usage des jeunes étudiants et des gens du monde, renfermant des considérations nouvelles sur les littératures ancienne et du moyen-âge, et

www.ingramcontent.com/pod-product-compliance
Lightning Source LLC
Chambersburg PA
CBHW070608100426
42744CB00006B/427